MODERN NOVELISTS

General Editor: Norman Page

Modern Novelists

MODERN NOVELISTS

CHRISTOPHER ISHERWOOD

Stephen Wade

St. Martin's Press   New York

Contents

© Stephen Wade 1991

First published in the United States of America in 1991

Printed in Hong Kong

Library of Congress Cataloging-in-Publication Data
Wade, Stephen, 1948–
Christopher Isherwood/Stephen Wade.
p.   cm. — (Modern novelists)
Includes bibliographical references and index.
ISBN 0-312-06040-8
1. Isherwood, Christopher, 1904–   —Criticism and interpretation.
I. Title.   II. Series.
PR6017.S5Z89   1991   90–24556
823'.912—dc20   CIP

For Cathy

For Colin

General Editor's Preface

The death of the novel has often been announced, and part of the secret of its obstinate vitality must be its capacity for growth, adaptation, self-renewal and even self-transformation: like some vigorous organism in a speeded-up Darwinian ecosystem, it adapts itself quickly to a changing world. War and revolution, economic crisis and social change, radically new ideologies such as Marxism and Freudianism, have made this century unprecedented in human history in the speed and extent of change, but the novel has shown an extraordinary capacity to find new forms and techniques and to accommodate new ideas and conceptions of human nature and human experience, and even to take up new positions on the nature of fiction itself.

In the generations immediately preceding and following 1914, the novel underwent a radical redefinition of its nature and possibilities. The present series of monographs is devoted to the novelists who created the modern novel and to those who, in their turn, either continued and extended, or reacted against the rejected, the traditions established during that period of intense exploration and experiment. It includes a number of those who lived and wrote in the nineteenth century but whose innovative contribution to the art of fiction makes it impossible to ignore them in any account of the origins of the modern novel; it also includes the so-called 'modernists' and those who in the mid and later twentieth century have emerged as outstanding practitioners in this genre. The scope is, inevitably, international; not only, in the migratory and exile-haunted world of our century, do writers refuse to heed national frontiers – 'English' literature lays claims to Conrad and Pole, Henry James the American, and Joyce the Irishman – but geniuses such as Flaubert, Dostoevsky and Kafka have had an influence on the fiction of many nations.

Each volume in the series is intended to provide an introduction to the fiction of the writer concerned, both for those approaching him or her for the first time and for those who are already familiar with some parts of the achievement in question and now wish to place it in the context of the total *oeuvre*. Although essential information relating to the writer's life and times is given, usually in an opening chapter, the approach is primarily critical and the emphasis is not upon 'background' or generalisations but upon close examination of important texts. Where an author is notably prolific, major texts have been selected for detailed attention but an attempt has also been made to convey, more summarily, a sense of the nature and quality of the author's work as a whole. Those who want to read further will find suggestions in the select bibliography included in each volume. Many novelists are, of course, not only novelists but also poets, essayists, biographers, dramatists, travel writers and so forth; many have practised shorter forms of fiction; and many have written letters or kept diaries that constitute a significant part of their literary output. A brief study cannot hope to deal with all these in detail, but where the shorter fiction and the non-fictional writings, public and private, have an important relationship to the novels, some space has been devoted to them.

NORMAN PAGE

1
Isherwood's Life and Work

The boundaries between autobiography and fiction in Isherwood's work are so blurred that a complete chapter of this book has been devoted to that topic. The autobiographical factors in any study of his writing involve principally his revolt against the values of his wealthy, well-established Cheshire family, his homosexuality and his firm religious beliefs. All of these figure prominently in his major novels and in all of his diverse writings. Apart from his fiction, Isherwood wrote plays (in collaboration with W. H. Auden), travel books, essays and translations. Most of these have some relevance to his novels but they will be dealt with only briefly in this introduction to his work.

This chapter summarizes the important phases in his long and busy life in literature, tracing his struggle for purpose, independence and, above all, artistic and religious fulfilment. His literary reputation rests mainly on his stories of Berlin during the rise of Hitler, but I hope to show that the fiction written later in his life, in America, has a great deal to interest the student of the modern novel, and is of considerable importance in terms of how novelists have written about religious experience.

From School to First Novel

Christopher William Bradshaw-Isherwood was born on 26 August 1904, at Wyberslegh, Cheshire. In his book *Kathleen and Frank* he has given a detailed account of his childhood and family life, using extensive diary entries and letters. His nanny was perhaps more prominent in his early life than his parents, and he reacted against the forceful character of his mother with a strong will to become independent and individual. His mother, Kathleen, was to figure in fictional guise in his early

1

work, and in certain ways came to represent the values of the older generation who had led Europe into the Great War. The nature of his pre-school years, however, is marked by his fascination with theatre and his involvement in a programme of education set out by his father, all these factors serving to make Christopher highly imaginative and also self-sufficient. His sense of drama and play was cultivated early, and perhaps explains his facility with dialogue in his writing. His mother was usually closely involved with the creative play:

> Dressing up meant the excitement and safety of disguise. You had to transform yourself as much as possible, so it was natural that you should change your sex. Kathleen didn't discourage this at all ...[1]

In 1914 he went to St Edmund's Preparatory School, Hindhead, and so began the first friendship in a long series of formative relationships throughout his childhood and youth: the meeting with W. H. Auden. Auden was precocious and eccentric, a strong personality with whom Isherwood attempted a collaboration – at least a design for a joint work – but it never materialized. The friendship was to be closer later on, after Repton, a public school in the Midlands, where Isherwood went in 1919. His autobiographical book *Lions and Shadows* contains a full account of the regime there, and the most profound influence on his development was from the enterprising history teacher G. B. Smith (Mr Holmes in the book).

Another close friend, Edward Upward, was also at Repton, and throughout Isherwood's life, Upward was to be the first consultant in writing matters. Together, they developed a private, anti-establishment, mythic world; one in which their rebellion and resentments could be expressed in creative, cathartic form. Incidentally, of course, the enterprise was to provide Isherwood with the initial training in characterization and structure that a young novelist needs.

It was at Repton that he became acutely aware of the rift between the 'hearties' and the more sensitive or academic students, and he and Upward coined the word 'Poshocracy' for the wealthy, hedonistic and athletic elements in the system. Their private anti-world had satire and caricature directed against such people and their attitudes, but the rift was even deeper in Isherwood's consciousness: it had a connection with his other preoccupation of 'The Test'. This was the manly, nationalistic code of ethics that had led thousands to their needless deaths in the trenches of the Great War. His own father had died, and the machismo aspects of school life came to be equated with notions of heroism and to be viewed as a kind of weakness:

> Like most of my generation, I was obsessed by a complex of terrors and longings connected with the idea 'War'. 'War' in the purely neurotic sense, meant The Test. The Test of your courage, of your maturity, of your sexual prowess; 'Are you really a man?' Subconsciously, I believe, I longed to be subjected to this test; but I also dreaded failure.[2]

Eventually, he and Upward came to the opinion that the Truly Weak Man was the one who had to take the Test and prove his manliness. These ideas were fully developed when Christopher entered Upward's college, Corpus Christi, in October 1923. Clearly, these preoccupations were related to Isherwood's uncertain position regarding accepted attitudes, morality and behaviour. He was a homosexual, interested in art and literature, struggling for independence from his mother who wanted him to be a university don or something of similar status. His private world of the imagination, Mortmere, like the Brontës' Gondal and Angria, provided an arena for the conflict of the emerging self-identity with the family and with authority.

He also cultivated the self-image of a defiant artist in a world of philistines: his diary-keeping was disciplined and detailed (as it was to be all his life) and provided material for future fiction. 'Isherwood the artist was an austere ascetic, cut off from the outside world, in voluntary exile, a recluse.'[3] He had literary heroes: Emily Brontë, Wilfred Owen, Katherine Mansfield and Baudelaire.

When this persona had been developed and nurtured, living life as if it were a work of art (as Wilde suggested), it was only natural that Mortmere became more prominent. The anti-world began to be written down and elaborated by Isherwood and Upward. They delighted in the expressive, surreal language that gave the fantasy 'a local habitation and a name':

> We wondered what the village should be called: Rats' Hall . . .
> Stoat Grange . . . Grangemere . . . Moatpool . . . Mortpool –

sounds too much like Blackpool. What a pity Mortlake's a real place – I've got it! Mortmere![4]

What is most evident in Mortmere, from a critical viewpoint, is the remarkable planning and character designing that was undertaken: 'Welkin's most intimate friend was Ronald Gunball, a frank, unashamed vulgarian, a keen fisherman, a drunkard and a grotesque liar.'[5] The stories were bizarre, surreal and boyishly indulgent, but what they did for Isherwood the novelist was to provide a stimulus for the writing of satirical and ironical fiction tinged with self-mockery and with central characters of great charm and magnetism, as the future Mr Norris or Uncle Lancaster were to be. Above all, this was a corrupt, seedy, daunting milieu for characters composed of their literary heroes' people and of the 'Poshocracy'. The one published story from this, Edward Upward's *The Railway Accident* (1969), shows the strengths of this individual, quirky narrative when it did fully cohere.

At Cambridge, where all this activity was intensified because of the dullness of the constitutional history course and the general revolt against the academic life, Isherwood began to attempt writing with the intention of participating in the exciting world of literature which had been revealed to him by experiences as diverse as I. A. Richards's lecture of modern poetry, Auden's enthusiasm for avant-garde writing and the reading of popular fiction. Naturally, the experience of the post-war generation had been reflected in the novels of the period; in many varied forms and styles. Isherwood was aware that he had experienced typical sorrows or traumas that could be communicated, and that his ruminations on The Test and on the Truly Weak Man were related to a common feeling of guilt and inadequacy that was experienced by men of his age, as they had somehow missed out on the great event of the 'war to end all wars':

The sense of an opportunity lost, of the test that one had failed without even having taken it, is expressed in many memories of the time, and is ... an important factor in the collective consciousness of the whole generation of young men who came of age between the wars.[6]

There is no doubt that his various forms of dissent were intensified. His main expression of this was in his increasing interest in serious fiction, in this case autobiographical works. The customary *Bildungsroman* of so many aspiring novelists was planned; it was to be called *Christopher Garland* and the summary of this work gives a valuable insight into his thoughts at this time:

> The story opens with the arrival of the young man after his last term at school; goes on to his first great period of inspiration, while staying in Sussex. Then comes Cambridge, with its terrible stupefying effect on the brain and spirit. In the vacation, the young man, cut off from his friends by his perceptions but not yet fully initiate, drifts into a dismal struggle with the personality of the aunt with whom he lives ....[7]

Isherwood realized all the shortcomings of this synopsis and everything that it suggested about his lofty ideals about art: he criticized the entire conception as not being 'rooted in life'. He was becoming increasingly committed to his writing, rather than to his degree studies. He and Upward decided that the best gesture would be to admit that the studious regime was not for them and, accordingly, this course of action was adopted:

> I must actually go into the examination room and write my insults as answers to the questions. The examining body itself would see them: they couldn't possibly be ignored ... Chalmers laughed riotously. He hadn't, as yet, the least suspicion that this wasn't just one more of a thousand fantastic anti-Cambridge plots.[8]

He achieved this, and left university in spring 1925, leaving himself aimless and prepared to consider various options. His writing, however, was being maintained, and a new draft of a novel emerged, called *Seascape with Figures*. It was rejected, but a friend advised him to persist and he hatched grand designs for novels of epic proportions. There was clearly the necessary dedication and seriousness in him, and in addition, he was enthusiastic to participate in the literary innovations that were so typical of the time. Plot and structure always had a fascination for him; he rarely ignored speculation and enquiry into new and adventurous ways of presenting narrative. *Seascape* became *All the Conspirators* and in 1927 that was submitted to publishers, and was in print by May 1928. This was indeed a watershed: he now had confidence and a belief in his ability. The successful first novel (though not commercially so) had been a questioning of the relationship with his mother, the pulls of tradition and morality, and also was a study of himself as an artist. The first stage in a long writing life that became increasingly preoccupied with the nature of self-identity had begun.

After a brief and unsuccessful attempt to pursue medical studies, the call of travel, particularly to Europe, had become too strong to resist. Auden had extolled the virtues of exciting, amoral, bohemian Berlin. He explained the psychological theories of Homer Lane, whose ideas appealed to young men from wealthy middle-class families who had a need for freedom and experimentation in life-styles and cultures which had more tolerance of non-heterosexual inclinations. Isherwood determined to move to Berlin; his second novel, *The Memorial*, was completed and published in 1932. He was growing to maturity intellectually; he needed a challenge and some artistic stimulation.

Still looking intensely into himself, he was acutely aware of his limitations, posturings and insecurities, all of which were to add depth and effectiveness to his 'Herr Issyvoo' narrator of the Berlin stories:

> I hadn't advanced an inch, really, since those Cambridge days. 'Isherwood the Artist' was still striking an attitude on his lonely rock. But his black Byronic exile's cloak failed to impress me any longer. I knew what was inside it now – just plain, cold, uninteresting funk. Funk of getting too deeply involved with other people, sex-funk, funk of the future.[9]

He was fundamentally insecure, but possibilities as to the fulfilment of his literary ambitions were real. He sensed that he was an important member of a group of writers and artists who could create a new kind of literature. Auden and Stephen Spender particularly shared this sense of purpose. The writer was seen as politically and socially involved; documentary realism was growing; a 'purpose' in a novel was admired, and it was an era of social parables and profound involvement in allegorical

'message' in the arts. The time was ripe for a writer with the
ability to write objectively about the important locations in contemporary European history. Isherwood went to Berlin with
little knowledge of what was to come in terms of his progress as a
novelist.

His steady but deeply felt revolt against the older generation,
The Test, conventional heterosexual morality, authority and
academicism, had been a creative force in his early life, as had
the intelligence and the ability to create readable and perceptive
social realism in his first novels. It also had another consequence
which Spender expresses well, referring to a similar revolt in his
own life:

> My revolt against the attitude of my family led me to rebel
> altogether against morality, work and discipline. Secretly I
> was fascinated by the worthless outcasts, the depraved, the
> lazy, the lost ....[10]

At the end of the 20s, many of the innovators of Modernism
such as Virginia Woolf and James Joyce had had their effect on
younger writers, and this interest in technique also coincided
with a glut of endlessly appealing subjects for fiction. The Great
War and the labour and financial crises had led to much writing
about class, snobbery, amorality and the aimless hedonism of
the Jazz Age. Evelyn Waugh and Aldous Huxley particularly
had perceived and commented on these trends: Isherwood
merely wrote about the elements in these social tendencies that
he knew most about from hard experience or from sensitivity. In
his first two novels he describes the unease and the angst of the
people who are the Truly Weak Men of The Test and the directionless perplexity of the younger ones such as himself and his
peers at prep school.

In the early 30s many developments in art, literature and
society influenced his intentions as a writer, but first he had to
learn more than the German language as he became a Berliner:
he had to encounter and try to comprehend the emergence of
Nazism and the decadence of Weimar Berlin. He also had to
learn many truths about himself, and to revise his concepts of
what a writer should be. Many of these issues and motivations
were discussed and explained in his autobiographical book
Lions and Shadows in 1938.

Berlin

In *Christopher and his Kind* (1977), Isherwood examines his period in Berlin in a revisionist fashion:

> However, when *Lions and Shadows* suggests that Christopher's chief motive for going to Berlin was that he wanted to meet Layard, it is avoiding the truth. He did look forward to meeting Layard, but that wasn't why he was in such a hurry to make his journey. It was Berlin itself he was hungry to meet; the Berlin Wystan had promised him. To Christopher, Berlin meant boys.[11]

Earlier, the mention of Layard (a follower of Homer Lane) had not involved any attempt to link his psychological ideas about freedom and individualism specifically to the homosexual interests of Auden and himself. However, a brief look at the Berlin to which he came in May 1929 does help to explain why Isherwood chose to live and write there after his abortive attempts to find a career in England. 'Boys' were an element of this, but there were many reasons.

Berlin was commonly seen as a focal point of European artistic, bohemian culture. It was considered to be dangerously amoral and avant-garde in attitudes. From its artistic community had come the theatre of Brecht, the vigour and freshness of Expressionism, cabaret satire, experimentation in the visual arts and generally a youthful, vital literature and art with a keen awareness of the context of mass unemployment and post-war depression. It was a city that had only recently experienced a revolution and fighting in the streets. Even if its reputation of open-minded tolerance of sexual deviation had been a dominant factor in Isherwood's choice, he could not have been unaware of these other aspects.

Otto Friedrich explains this cultural and artistic richness very vividly, referring to the times called 'Die goldenen zwanziger Jahre' (The Golden Twenties):

> The twenties were not golden for everyone, of course, for these were the years of the great inflation, of strikes and riots, unemployment and bankruptcy, and Nazis and Communists battling in the streets. Still, the magic names kept recurring – Marlene Dietrich, Garbo, Baker, the grandiose productions

of Max Reinhardt's "Theatre of the 5000", three opera com-
panies running under Walter, Klemperer and Kleiber . . . .
Almost overnight, the somewhat staid capital of Kaiser Wil-
helm had become the centre of Europe. Above all, Berlin in
the twenties represented a state of mind, a sense of freedom
and exhilaration.[12]

For a young English writer, this 'state of mind' was combined
with the situation described by Kenneth Tynan: 'Socialism and
self-gratification at the same time'[13] and there was the deeper
level at which Berlin affected its inhabitants. This concerned the
tensions and oppositions within the city which seemed then to be
a microcosm of Europe under the growth of Fascism. Peter
Vansittart expresses this well:

> For many, perhaps most of us, the thirties seemed to have
> induced moral and political simplicity, surprising in an age
> that readily gulped down Freud. Exciting opposites forbade
> neutrality. Decency fought Terror . . . Left was against Right,
> notably in Weimar Germany, where Reds and Blacks could
> unite in strikes to weaken the Social Democratic Republic.[14]

There was this conflict and tension almost everywhere, but beneath the pretences and distractions. Spender writes, 'The feeling of unrest in Berlin went deeper than any crisis. It was a
permanent unrest, the result of nothing being fixed and
settled.'[15]

It requires some effort of imagination to comprehend Isherwood and Spender living within this milieu, but many events and
tendencies explain the dozens of social elements that contrib-
uted to the fine achievements of the Berlin stories and to *Mr
Norris Changes Trains* (1935) and *Sally Bowles* (1937). Spender
has commented on one main characteristic of their lives there:

> Christopher and I, leading our lives in which we used Ger-
> many as a kind of cure for our personal problems, became
> ever more aware that the carefree personal lives of our friends
> were facades in front of the immense social chaos.
>   There was more and more a feeling that this life would be
> swept away.[16]

This unrest, uncertainty and conflict was to be the broad canvas of the Berlin writing, but there was another side to life there which was to be an essential ingredient of a massive projected novel called *The Lost* which Isherwood described to John Lehmann at the time. This concerns, in the most part, the working classes. In Berlin, with 4 000 000 inhabitants, there were 750 000 unemployed, walking in the forests, settling in camps, often hungry and haunting the cafes and bars. The image of the proletarian had to be a part of the picture that conveyed acknowledgement and respect. Even Bertold Brecht absorbed this and cultivated the proletarian in his own dress and image.[17]

Isherwood's situation, then, on arriving in Berlin, was that his first novel was published but commercially a failure. The book had been remaindered. Critically, its reception had been neutral but some admiration had been expressed. His life in Berlin was hard but the 'education of the streets' was perfect for a novelist in search of material. Spender knew him well at this time:

> During the years when I was often in Berlin, he lived in various poor parts of the town, of which the best was in the neighbourhood of the Nollendorfplatz – a grand-shabby square . . . the worst, the Hallesches Tor, an area of slum tenements. He lived very poorly, scarcely ever spending more than sixty pfennigs (about eightpence) on a meal. We ate food such as horse flesh and lung soup.[18]

Isherwood later commented that he was 'the only one there', and that he was 'the only English-speaking writer to write a book about that period . . . those stories created a world. (Readers) like to be able to see people's whole lives as though they were in a fishbowl'.[19] His literary reputation still rests largely on the writing about 30s Berlin, and the reason for this is partly that his unique fusing of social documentary realism and ironic characterization was a highly successful formula which was later crystallized in the film *Cabaret*. His unfailing ability to give life to characters who exist powerfully as individuals and yet give enlightenment in matters of politics or morals is the fundamental explanation of his success.

It was in this period that he began to communicate with John Lehmann about the publishing of a new type of book-magazine: one that would combine the twin functions of a forum for new writers and of addressing itself to questions of contemporary history in the spirit of the recent trend towards realistic documentary art and literature. This was to become *New Writing*, a publication that helped many talented 30s writers to find their audience. Lehmann has written a great deal about his close contact with Isherwood at this time, notably in a recent memoir.[20] In 1940, however, with the impact of the Berlin stories' success as a collection the previous year, he summed up Isherwood's status and aims at the time:

> *The Nowaks*, by general consent one of the finest long short-stories that have been written since the last war, followed *Mr Norris* in the first number of *New Writing* in the autumn of 1936 .... Isherwood's original idea was to write one long novel, a panorama of Berlin life in the five years which preceded the Nazis' seizure of power ....[21]

The plan never materialized, but the various stories give insights into the ordinary lives of Berliners at the time, and depict a world of contradictions and conflicts, divisions and compromises, with sharp irony and dark humour. Lehmann sees the Berlin Isherwood as a moralist – 'One who is aware of, and in the deepest layer of his nature condemns, social injustice and the phenomenon of social decay, and sees that there are forces emerging in the pattern of history to challenge them.'[22] When he left Berlin in May 1933 he had produced only a small body of work in comparison with his overall aims, but there was a great deal of potential material recorded in notebooks and journals.

This startling originality and the various influences on his writing made his participation in *New Writing* extremely significant: both for his career and for the magazine's progress. He was to continue writing for this influential magazine even after his move to America.

Realism and Reportage

In Lehmann's magazine, a section headed 'The Living Moment' dealt with contemporary accounts of work and workers, social class, autobiography and wartime experiences. This was in keeping with the urge to write what we would now call 'faction':

reportage was infiltrating literature and had done so since it became particularly urgent that working-class experience should have a voice. The Spanish Civil War of 1936 had played an important part in this, as many working-class Englishmen had participated in it. Also George Orwell's writings about the poor in Paris and in London had awakened interest in the lower classes as subjects for the novelist.

Isherwood is invariably discussed in this context, in which Auden could write a poem as commentary for the GPO film *Night Mail* and readers clamoured for firsthand accounts of proletarian life. The interest of the 1930s writers in politics, in the nature of a writer's commitment and in the factual reporting of events was significant: the worker-writer became increasingly common and often in terms of open contradistinction to the rarefied Bloomsbury intellectualism. B. L. Coombes, for instance, was a South Wales miner who was published in *New Writing*, and his subject of a miner's life was fresh, direct and, above all, informative. This was the age of Mass Observation, the documentary of ordinary, everyday life-style and opinion; it was also the decade in which Gollancz's Left Book Club published accounts of contemporary life and politics in great detail.

It has often been too easily assumed that the Berlin fiction is to be compartmentalized with these writings and with the documentary approach, but there is much truth in Gustav Klaus' comments on this:

> In Isherwood's case, this sensibility takes on a strongly private character .... One is left with a sense that, in a different situation, where the grip of the political sphere on personal life was less pervasive ... the author would have devoted himself entirely to the realm of the private.[23]

In an interview, Isherwood also challenges the common use of the term 'Camera Eye' with regard to his approach. He had been strongly influenced by film technique, and he did feel the attraction of *New Writing*'s particular style, but his comment in the interview is worth consideration:

> This business about being a camera is very misleading. As I've often had occasion to point out, what I really meant by saying, "I am a camera," was *not* I am a camera all the time, and that

I'm like a camera. It was: I'm in the strangest mood at this particular moment ... I just sit and register impressions through the window – visual data – without any reaction to it, like a camera. The idea that I was a person divorced from what was going on around me is quite false.[24]

Any judgement of his 1930s writings has, therefore, to be cautious in this context: it is too easy to compare the account of Mr Norris at the workers' meeting with a section of Orwell such as the hop-picking in Kent (*The Clergyman's Daughter*). Isherwood's focus is usually on the narrator-protagonist rapport and on the consequent irony than on the exterior, tangential reportage where the intention is a didactic mode of writing, as is found in long episodes of Orwell's fiction.

The other aspects of his life and sense of purpose were gaining momentum in this period: principally the sexual fulfilment, the search for independence and the intense concern for 'Isherwood the Artist' – the cultivated persona that had its origins in his life at Cambridge. In all his later autobiographical works he differentiates the 'Christopher' from the 'I' in the narrative. These tensions were creative in art, but problematic in life. He needed self-discipline and a fresh challenge, away from the intensely self-preoccupied world of his Berlin ambience.

His chance came when he and Auden were commissioned to write a book on the Sino-Japanese War in Manchuria, *Journey to a War* (1939), and he also collaborated with Auden in the plays *The Dog Beneath the Skin* (1935) and *The Ascent of F6* (1936). Throughout the late 30s he and Auden had wandered about Europe – experience that would be used in later novels – and, after the war book, America beckoned to them both. The departure of Auden and Isherwood for the USA shortly before the Second World War was described by Cyril Connolly as the most significant event since the Spanish Civil War: Evelyn Waugh expressed the more general view when he poked fun at them, as Parsnip and Pimpernel in *Put Out More Flags*. But for Isherwood, the break with Europe meant a restless, self-questioning period in which he reflected and philosophized, particularly on pacifism (as his German lover Heinz, from whom he had been forced to part, could have been his enemy if Isherwood had participated in the war).

Only one novel was written in the period up to his interest in

Vedanta Hinduism (1939–54): *Prater Violet* (1945) and this takes up the familiar techniques of detachment, comic irony and reliance on one focal ego in the narrative: but at the conclusion there is a hint of the writing about religious experience, belief and self-identity that was to come. He writes about his worries and apprehensions and about how the individual should find a way to overcome these anxieties.

Homosexuality

In studying Isherwood's novels, one fundamental point has to be made in a general survey: his homosexuality adds a particular dimension to his fiction. The homosexual writer views conventional, heterosexual morality and behaviour in a specific way: seeing with acuteness and sensitivity the influences and patterns of morality and authority in the normal family structure. Isherwood's efforts to understand his mother's profound influence on him, and his fictional account of the failures of machismo codes of honour (in *The Memorial*) gradually led him towards an honesty in the expression of the nature of his self – a recognition of 'I' as well as 'Christopher the Artist'. Mr Norris is merely a stereotype in the generally accepted potrayal of effeminacy: arch, untrustworthy, whimsical and dangerous to know. Bergmann, in *Prater Violet*, is passionate and open in his feelings. The difference in the two characters pinpoints the nature of the changes taking place in Isherwood's attitudes to homosexuality in his post-war fiction.

Also, one must not overlook the legality and morality involved in the publishing of overtly homosexual fiction: E. M. Forster's *Maurice* did not appear in print until 1971, though it had been written in 1914. The more open-minded attitudes of today may make one forget earlier viewpoints. Quentin Crisp explains the changes well: 'In an expanding universe, time is on the side of the outcast. Those who once inhabited the suburbs of human contempt find that without changing their address they eventually live in the metropolis.'[25]

In the 1930s, however, sex, according to several writers at the time, was an *idée fixe* in art and literature. Louis MacNeice, for example, explained that this 'obsession with sex' led to 'the failure in our time of so many movements both in the arts and in public life. We were a nation of sexual frustrates.'[26] When Isherwood went to Berlin, it was, as already suggested, in search of 'boys' but there was also the fascination with the entire atmosphere: Berlin had the Hirschfeld Institute for sexual research and the whole milieu had dark suggestions of perversion and deviation, material used in the episodes where Mr Norris is linked with masochism and sadistic sex.

It was only when he settled in California that he moved away from the preoccupation with working-class boys that was often written about in 30s novels,[27] and he also found that the nature of homosexuality as social taboo was not apparent there. California was where expatriate Europeans often settled; there was the film community, gay subculture and more latitude in artistic as well as sexual endeavour and an attractive climate. He worked there on filmscripts, discovered Vedanta and worked steadily on his novels: works which explored these themes of religious experience and homosexuality in a variety of ways. He made a stable and close relationship with the artist, Don Bachardy, and found that such fulfilment influenced, in a positive way, his attitude to writing about homosexual relationships.

Vedanta

Increasingly, a preoccupation with the philosophical and religious dimensions of life led Isherwood into the company of strongly individual intellectuals: Aldous Huxley and Gerald Heard, a charismatic pacifist who attracted many disciples, in particular provoked much thought. Isherwood settled in California to be with them in 1939. Even more important for the course his life was to take was his meeting with the Hindu guru Swami Prabhavananda. With him, Isherwood began the study of Vedanta philosophy and practised meditation techniques. The Swami was leading a community of the Ramakrishna order in Hollywood. Vedanta teaches that the materialist impedimenta of life and the concern with time are secondary to the important purpose of life: to know oneself and to love the creatures of the world. It is tolerant, passive and Quietist; as such it met Isherwood's pacifism and clarified his worries about the need for personal action of some kind. His regime and strenuous efforts towards self-discipline are recorded in *My Guru and His*

Disciple (1980) and clearly, some friends in England were bemused by and sceptical of this radical change in Isherwood's life. His Swami even accommodated Isherwood's sexual relationships with the humane and tolerant philosophy.

Such a change in life-style and self-awareness naturally effected significant developments in his fiction. Four novels deal with different aspects of his life and beliefs at the time, and two of these deal specifically with homosexual love in addition to the religious perspectives. But the subject that Isherwood really considered in the last phase of his career was the problem of writing a novel on a religious subject: how could (or should) one explain religious insights in the medium of words – a medium doomed to be inadequate?

He also approached this question in many autobiographical writings, mostly based on copious diaries. Within these works, he takes the reader through the stages of conversion and expresses a sense of the immediacy and complexity of his struggle for self-understanding. One of these passages about the nature of Vedanta is typical of the challenge of so many new concepts with which his intellect and emotions were dealing at the time:

> Prabhavananda explained that Brahmananda didn't love others in a person to person way. Having realised God, who is love, he had *become* love. Those who came into his presence felt that love; he gave forth love while remaining incapable of possessiveness or jealousy.[28]

Isherwood became more deeply involved in the disciplines and theories connected with a life of meditation, prayer and self-negation (in the worldly, material sense). It was only natural that his fiction should reflect this. He took on the editorship of *Vedanta and the West* in 1943. This was a magazine covering issues and topics connected with the theory and practice of Vedanta teachings and their relevance to Western intellectual life. He was also involved in peace studies and in teaching, and he wrote a travel book, *The Condor and the Cows* (1948). Unchanged amid all this, however, was his need to pursue a life that would relate to his new beliefs: the new Christopher and the re-emerging persona in the later novels were products of this.

Obviously, during the years when his religious novels were

written, views of his work were coloured by concurrent developments in American literature such as the work of Ginsberg and
the Beat Poets, Jack Kerouac,[29] the rediscovery of the writings
of Herman Hesse and the newer forms of transcendental writing. Yet Isherwood was only peripheral in this context. He per-
sisted in his own novelistic aims, determinedly keeping to the
path that he had set himself to follow.

His literary friends tried to understand; Lehmann, in a recent
book, writes in a way that almost suggests that the conversion to
Vedanta was inexplicable unless one fully empathized with
Isherwood. What is easily demonstrable is that his life in
California, where he eventually settled in Santa Monica with
Don Bachardy, was intensely stimulating and fulfilling. The
essays, interviews and fiction, together with a large output of
autobiography, all reflect a life of curiosity, intellectual enterprise and profound reflection. There is ample evidence that the
four last novels were designed and executed in terms of far more
thoughtful theory and purpose than the Berlin fiction. Most of
the central preoccupations of these American novels have influential factors that embrace subjects of minorities, homosexual mores, pacifism, commitment, the experience of
bereavement, education, religious experience and many more.
A critic has to see him, in certain respects, as an American
writer foremost: yet there are clear limitations, principally with
regard to the past, in this approach.[30]

Christopher Isherwood continued thinking, working and
practising Vedanta Hinduism until his death in 1985, in California, where he had lived for 45 years. He had been a prominent
figure in the history of the English novel in two significant
periods: the first, approximately 1932 to 1939, in an era of documentary and allegory, and the second (1954 to 1969) in a time of
sexual liberation and intense individualistic expression.

2

Early Novels

There are many influences at work behind *All the Conspirators* (1928) and *The Memorial* (1932), Isherwood's first two novels. They were produced in a period of intense self-questioning, rebellion against established middle-class mores, and adaptation to his homosexuality in the world outside school and Cambridge. Both are based in autobiography, making use of the Bradshaw family, the strong personality of his mother, and of the extreme dislike felt by Upward and himself for the Cambridge 'Hearties'. However evident these aspects may be, the novels are significant achievements for a young man with an apparently narrow education. This narrowness and typicality was perhaps the secret of their artistic success. He had experienced public school and Cambridge life and regimes at a time when his generation felt the sense of having missed the chance to 'prove' themselves for their country. In addition, he wrote about his generation's malaise by expressing his own with vigour, variety and the right balance of experimentation and modernity in style and language.

The young novelist may be observed practising technique, enjoying satire and, most prominently, studying his own dilemma. Both novels explore elements of his complex situation in 1927–32, covering the time of his medical studies and his early period in Berlin. Very little from life is omitted in fiction. Isherwood makes fictional use of his disastrous and abortive study of medicine at King's College; his experience of the Cambridge 'Blue' and philistine; the nature of the rift with his mother and the increasing prominence of his homosexuality in his life. There had also been a succession of failures and questionings. He had failed as a scholar, as a medical student and as a son. He had also failed to conform, both to family morality and to career-orientation. There was much to be confronted in art that could not be understood or achieved in life, and he simply needed the correct form of fiction in order to help in self-understanding and in clarifying the situation.

All the Conspirators is undoubtedly a novel of great vitality and invention. When the small-scale, domestic nature of the subject-matter is noted, the novel's interest and readability is all the more remarkable. It is, substantially, the story of a revolt against authority and an assertion of self that only succeeds in terms of an acceptable defeat. Isherwood, in a preface written to the 1957 edition, takes an objective view of his first novel and is critical of the technique, speaking of himself in the third person:

> But the echoes of James Joyce annoy me, because they are merely echoes. I find this repeated use of the Joycean thought-stream technique jarringly out of style. Its self-consciously grim, sardonically detached tone doesn't suit any of the characters; even coming from Allen Chalmers it rings false.[1]

He also tackles the 'obscurity', by which he means elements of style and language which have their origin in his and Upward's Mortmere and with an idiosyncratic humour:

> I now detect a great deal of aggression in this kind of obscurity. Young writers are apt to employ it as a secret language which is intelligible only to their friends, the members of their group. Outsiders, including all professional critics, are thereby challenged to admit that they don't understand it or dared to pretend that they do.[2]

Nevertheless, with or without knowledge of Isherwood's biography, the reader will find the novel rich in perceptions of the unease and dissent of the generation coming to maturity in the late twenties, many of whom had found their parents' attitudes to conventional morality and religion to be wrong-headed and simplistic. As Philip Larkin commented about 1914: 'Never such innocence again'.[3] In the case of the mother-figure of this novel, her 'innocence' is in believing that all is well if one fulfils role-models and expectations based on convention and on solid bourgeois values.

Isherwood's preface undervalues his achievement here. The

'obscurity' is only rarely openly indulgent – in the contempt of the minutiae of his education and friendships. Mostly, it expresses itself in merciless satire, subtle irony and a zestful wit, owing something to Oscar Wilde. Sometimes, the metaphors are too artificial and adventurous, but when they work, the effect is impressive. Above all else, the strength of the novel is in the consummate use of dialogue, which was always a fundamental strength in his work.

As mentioned previously, he had been experimenting, absorbing technique and sense of structure for many years before this first success. Many formative influences have been isolated and discussed, but none more so than E. M. Forster's 'tea-tabling' approach. This is basically the use of understatement and the power of ironies developing from apparently trivial, mundane events:

> Forster's 'tea-tabling' meant much more than a mere device to him. It profoundly affected his moral vision. By deliberately underplaying scenes and events in *All the Conspirators* which the traditional Edwardian novel would have treated as most significant, Isherwood was able to subtly undermine conventional moral values even while the narrative was ostensibly tracing their triumph over a younger generation's unsuccessful revolt.[4]

The novel is about this kind of revolt, but just as much about the failed artist and failed personality Isherwood would have become if the writing life had not been viable. It is, in other words, a novel concerned with moral cowardice, and as Isherwood himself studies this in a persona, Philip Lindsay, it is a novel that contains some frank self-scrutiny beneath the veneer of verbal cleverness, inner monologue and flashback.

Philip and his friend, Allan Chalmers, discuss art in the opening chapters, and, in their Isle of Wight holiday environment, feel free to tease and denigrate Victor Page, a pipe-smoking Cambridge student with a military father and 'Hearty' attitudes. When we learn that Philip has given up his office job and is attempting to both write and paint and to rebel against his dominant mother, we see that it is a story of a play for freedom and a fight to maintain influence. Victor is encouraged to court Philip's sister, Joan, and they eventually become engaged.

Philip walks out again and has passed over a chance to work on Victor's father's coffee plantation in Kenya. His illness (rheumatic fever) enables him to return home to live the life of a pampered dilettante.

The life of the novel is in the constant interest that Isherwood creates in Philip's dilemma, in the ambivalence created towards him and in the wider discontent that he represents, even though his own story is one of ignominious failure. The vitality is in the sarcasm, irony and sheer domestic, internecine malevolence and duplicity: the masks of affection in the family relationships. Only in rare moments does the London setting impinge and, outside the Lindsay house, only Allen Chalmer's flat is used for the bulk of the novel (Chalmers is a medical student).

Isherwood maintains this ambivalence through the novel by establishing Philip initially as a serious artist, theorizing with real commitment and zeal. He also gives us the events and environment with conciseness and economy:

> "I rather prefer to tackle the subjects that you think ... obvious; and extract something from them.
> It's easy enough to be 'interesting' in your way."
> "And these 'genuine forms of life' that you extract things from include?"
> "Oh, if you want a catalogue – well, put it that I'm not AFRAID of anything. One's got to have the nerve – I want to do picture-postcard sunsets, cows crossing a stream ...."[5]

Consequently, the reader's belief in Philip is there to be gradually eroded as we judge his subsequent behaviour. Only cautiously do we admit the dilettantism in him.

He also has the requisite stinging wit and the love of hyperbole and innuendo that attracts a young generation in a mood for debunking:

> I'd rather hoped to get a room out somewhere. One can't work in the house. If mother isn't coming in and out with a duster to see whether the maids have been along the mantelpiece, there's Currants wanting to know a word of three letters meaning wicked.[6]

Most prominent in the presentation of Philip's character, however, is the effort that Isherwood makes to mix a specific satirical portrait with impressionistic statements of general application, as when he returns from holiday to a confrontation with his mother:

> He nodded. Suddenly, he had felt physically tired all over. It was as if they had already been talking for hours. He regarded her stupidly, intently, confused by irrelevant memories, associations suggested by the stair-carpet, the lithographs and the little rugs. A queer atrophy of the will. He thought: I'm being hypnotised.[7]

Mrs Lindsay's 'hypnotism' is that of the past; in her home, he is her young child. Just as her books and furniture represent the comfortable Edwardian middle class, so her effect on the adult Philip is to mesmerize him into that state and context: no change or progression is permitted under her roof.

The older generation as a whole are mercilessly attacked, and by irony: Mr Langbridge's letter of platitudinous advice, Colonel Page's arranging of the Kenya job and his mother's money-snobbery all shape the picture. In the most sustained and vitriolic satire of the novel, Victor is depicted as the gauche and blockish embodiment of all that is outrageous and despicable in the Cambridge philistine, and all that is weak in The Truly Weak Man. Isherwood's approach here is best explained by referring to the scene where Victor is engaged to marry Joan and is now being accepted into the family in a ritualistic way that both amuses and revolts Philip. Here, he has explained to Chalmers how this acceptance is a 'ballet' of actions and expected behaviour:

> What Philip vaguely meant was that Victor, when he came downstairs in the morning, kissed Mrs Lindsay on the cheek; that he stood up whenever Joan moved from her chair and was ready to open the door for her when she left the room; that he called Miss Durrant Currants and held her skeins of wool ... that he generally slapped Philip on the back whenever they met, and always came down to Philip's sitting-room after dinner to smoke a pipe ... to ask what books he ought to read. Something decent, I mean. One gets frightfully tired of shockers.[8]

In addition to the influence of Forster, the novel also gives ample evidence of Isherwood's absorption of film technique. There is perhaps also some suggestion here that he found sharp visual detail to be a powerful means of adding threat and essential information about motivation. Philip's panic, running into nocturnal London, buying a coat from a pawnbroker, finding a cheap hotel, and his subsequent collapse in the street, all show how Isherwood had learned the skill of giving informative detail deftly, with economy (Chapter 17 makes an effective short story in itself):

> Philip turned up his collar and stood for some minutes in the archway of a court. The place was full of children, swarming around in the gloom, dodging each other, falling over; uttering weird shrieks, like seagulls in a cave ....[9]

Philip's ultimate defeat recalls Chekhov's Uncle Vanya, forced to be reconciled to the mundane, the trivial and, above all, to the effort of maintaining a self-delusion in order that some form of life is to go on. In one sense, Philip's destination was always predictable: the cosiness and the maternal intrusion were far superior in resources and in potency to his artistic commitment. Even if he had gone to Kenya, it would still be a surrender to The Enemy and The Test. But the final version we have of The Truly Weak Man lives by a pretence as egregious and hollow as Victor's. Like Vanya, the only consolation left to Philip is that of the pathetic, comfortable self-deception of the failure who is able to exist in a life of pretence.

Turning to *The Memorial* (1932), which was conceived and planned as early as 1928, there is a significant development and a sense of mere ambition and confidence. When one considers the impact of T. S. Eliot's poem, *The Waste Land* (1922), which Isherwood himself mentions in his autobiographical work, *Lions and Shadows*, on the generation of the twenties and early thirties then it is easily observed that there were many versions of the literature of disillusion and the failure to live. As in Eliot's poem, many novels of the time show a society whose members feel the isolation and shock of a failed society which has undergone a stealthy revolution in morality and belief. Just as Evelyn Waugh and Aldous Huxley felt the need to express these perceptions of a diseased society, Isherwood, in this second novel, has a great deal to say about the roots of discontent.

For this reason, the experiments with technique and verbal wit and aphorism are much less prominent. He had a clear idea of his purpose:

> It was to be about war: not the war itself, but the effect of the idea of war on my generation. It was to give expression, at last, to my own 'war' complex, and to all the reactions which had followed my meeting with Lester at the Bay.[10]

The Bay is Freshwater Bay, and 'Lester' a suffering war veteran and victim of the trenches. In *Lions and Shadows* Isherwood also begins to discuss his aim of writing an 'epic', suggesting that he clearly felt confident enough to extract from his own limited experience, the necessary material to give an overview of various conditions and classes in the post-war society. Clearly, he often thought in these large-scale terms. Later, *The Lost* was to be a similar exploration of thirties Berlin. As is apparent in *The Memorial*, he was perceptive enough to realize that he was the kind of novelist who must avoid what he does not know at first hand. Hence, the proletarian issues are kept to a minimum, with Eric's interests in the South Wales miners and similar concerns being the only element of this. He keeps to what autobiographical elements from his own experience since the death of his father would be most significant and most universal, though never losing sight of the need to explore his own feelings too. Consequently, the novel deals with heroism and courage, bereavement, the aristocracy, artistic cliques and the officers who felt a sense of alienation at their sudden return to civilian life. The only episode which is not derived from first-hand knowledge is Edward Blake's attempted suicide, and even this is vividly and convincingly handled, showing how far he had progressed since the experiments of the first novel:

> A stab of pain like a hot lancet slid between his eyes. It had started. Edward uttered a groan and lay back, covering his face with his hands. The taxi swung to the right, to the left. He was, suddenly, horribly seasick, tried to put his head out of the window, failed, and vomited on the floor.[11]

The novel explores three central elements of post-war society: through Lily (the mother-figure again) there is loss and a vapid lack of purpose; in Blake we have the nature of manliness and courage, and finally, in Eric we have a composite personality of all the potentialities within Isherwood himself. At the time of writing the book, Isherwood obviously still felt the desire to resolve some of these issues to his own satisfaction, and the Modernist techniques used in *All the Conspirators* may have been impressive, but they only dealt superficially and one-sidedly with such things.

Another important feature of the second novel is its structure. The narrative unfolds with four settings in reordered time: a sequence of 1928, 1920, 1925 and 1929 enabling the reader to perceive motivations and consequences with clarity and interest. The principal benefit here is in the revelation of causes: in a novel concerned with inter-relationships and the establishment of individuality in a world of uncertain values, the causes of behaviour and attitudes must be given and presented to the reader in terms of intensive and realistic characterization. (It is interesting to note that William Faulkner's *The Sound and the Fury* (1929) gives a similar approach but using the first person.) Forster's 'tea-tabling' once more proved to be the most successful approach, with characters betraying themselves by actions and attitudes in a context which tests their open-mindedness and humanity.

There is also some degree of catharsis in the novel. The account of Eric's relationship with his mother, Lily, goes considerably deeper than the mother-son relationship of Philip and Dorothy Lindsay. Many episodes use experiences in Isherwood's relationships with both his parents, but particularly with his mother. He adds some fictional elements, such as Eric's stammer and his work with the poor, but essentially, it is a novel of catharsis and the resolution of doubts. It aims to reveal the hollowness and aimlessness, together with the moral and individual uncertainties of his peers and of his familial forebears. In the accounts of daily ritual, 'proper' conduct, dishonest reserve and mindless fulfilment of roles, he shows us a lost society, in search of meanings and purposes after a cataclysmic conflict.

The Memorial recounts the story of a family and its close friends, focusing on Lily Vernon, a war-widow, and her relationship with Eric, her over-protected, clever son. The story also enquires into the nature of courage and commitment to ideas and creeds, centrally in the person of Edward Blake, a soldier and one of the directionless young; also pinpointed in Maurice, Tom and Anne, with their circle of friends. Above all, what they all have in common is an unsure self-consciousness, a view of a social veneer, an appearance. Lily is shown as sadly contemplative of her own image in her mirror, in several episodes such as this:

> That evening Lily had knelt down in her dressing-gown with her elbows on the dressing-table, to get the full light of the candles burning on either side of the mirror. Opening the silk blotting-book, she continued her letter to her aunt: 'The house itself is partly Elizabethan ....'[12]

In this 1920 section, Isherwood writes at length about the local society in Cheshire where the Vernons are the squirearchy, and he makes the commemorative service and the Memorial itself into a representative account of the community in this post-war malaise, undergoing change and doubt, but still desperately in need of the ritual and comforts of traditional patterns of life and social, hierarchical order. When old Mr Vernon, Lily's father-in-law, attends the Memorial it is a scene that reveals this well when Vernon's actions at the service are described:

> Then he stood still for a moment, facing the Cross, perhaps uncertain what to do next. It was understood that he was praying. Father's ponderousness had had its usual effect upon his audience. They were impressed.[13]

The artificiality and emptiness of all the occurrences at the Memorial service assemble a picture of a society where the upper and lower echelons are equally vacuous. Lily is fussy, insistent on her rights and respects, complaining and selfishly assertive about privilege. Her profound influence on Eric is expressed in exactly the way that we find it put in later autobiographical works where Isherwood re-examines his childhood and youth:

> Darling Eric. He must fulfil what Richard would have wished. He must be a don. Everyone told her that he was so clever. His history master felt sure that he would get an entrance scholarship to Cambridge of course. How delightful that would be.

How happy it would make Richard. And Lily saw herself walking with her son, arm-in-arm, along the most beautiful parts of the Backs . . . .[14]

The selfishness and vanity in her form part of the overall impression that the older generation are still thoughtlessly struggling to maintain traditional virtues and aspirations, ignoring claims for individuality or significant change on the part of the young. Eric is torn between submission to her will and his own artistic impulses, and although his poetry and day-dreaming are often humorously presented, the really significant passage with regard to his nature comes at the end of the 1920 section, where much more is made of this. A poetic, fanciful thought gives rise to a metaphor that indicates his isolation and difference from the rest of the crowd of young people, and also gives us the symbolic focus of the Memorial itself. He is on his bicycle when the idea occurs to him:

> Chapel Bridge and Gatesley were like the two poles of a magnet. Chapel Bridge – the black asphalt and brick village, his village, clean, urban, dead – he called the negative pole. Gatesley – their village, lying so romantically in the narrow valley . . . that was the positive pole. If you rode over . . . you were like a pin on a bit of metal . . . but a pin would never move between the poles at all, but fly to one and stick there.[15]

The Memorial, his mother and the Hall pull at him, in his mind, restraining him from the open ground. The story goes on to chronicle his moves towards freedom. In the opening 1928 section, at dinner with his mother, he tires of the empty ceremony of tea and polite questions. Gatesley has won, and he is himself. The stammer recedes.

Perhaps the most vital and important character with regard to the effects of war is Blake, as he embodies The Truly Weak Man of Isherwood's theorizing with Upward at Repton and Cambridge. Isherwood capitalizes on the force of contrast, comparing Blake with Eric's father-hero, Richard. Richard had been 'sure of himself – therefore he did not have to fight and boast'[16] but Edward Blake has felt the call of The Test, proved to be a war hero in a romanticized context, and almost gains a V.C. Richard, on the other hand, has died. Thus he has had no ennui to deal with; no sense of displacement. The living Weak Man has to find an arena or perish:

> Edward had nothing but time. He fidgeted about town, dabbled and dawdled, could settle to nothing. From a seat in the park, from an armchair in his club, he regarded the enormous horizons which opened ... such horizons appalled him.[17]

Blake only finds distraction and entertainment with the younger group, impressing with his vigour, showmanship and childish sense of fun, but there is a glimpse of how deeply the military and manly Test goes in this type when Major Charlesworth, asked (in the final 1929 section) what he would change in his life if given the chance to relive, simply answers, 'I might have been better off in a cavalry regiment'.[18]

Charlesworth and Blake are examples of the soldiers of all ages who are unable to adapt to civilian life. They search for a purpose and meaning outside the rigidly-defined rules and expectations of the military life: one still searching for 'macho' justification, and the other in need of romance and human communication.

Throughout the novel, each person, group or ethos atrophies or declines, or even intensifies in neurosis and angst. It is bleak in terms of all-pervading melancholy and self-searching despair. In this respect, Eric and Edward form an interesting contrast as two sides of Isherwood and his potential conditions at that stage (c.1920) when so many possibilities arose. It has been pointed out that they are the first example of his idea of 'doubles' of his own self's projections and that they were part of a plan in which a man is 'a dream of himself as an epic character'.[19] Certainly, in *The Memorial*, both have ideals or myths to attain or serve. Blake is the representative of he who relies on stereotype ideals and constructs of ideology. Eric is partly the 'new man', with commitment to vital social action, though emasculated himself. Both are trapped in the ritual of expectations.

Other characters act 'parts' and align their lives with familiar ritual too: in the last section, this motif intensifies. Again, it seems that Forster's presence is detectable in the writing. Recurrent images or scenes of contrasting but complementary pretence, ritual or acting of roles occur. In the young people, the parlour games and charades, the parties and concerts are hollow distractions from importance and meaning. This is encapsulated in the following brief scene:

> "Mary as Queen Victoria" shouted everybody that evening at the Gowers', after the concert.
> "But you must all have seen it."
> "We all want to see it again."
> "Very well," said Mary, smiling, "Since you're all so kind. But this is really and truly the very, very last performance on any stage."
> "Liar!" Maurice shouted.[20]

Lily observes herself consciously, Eric stammers at every entrance and plays a role of philanthropist; Mary stages the events of the coterie; Edward has to maintain the war veteran image and Richard Vernon the part of squire. In the ultimate histrionic gesture, at the conclusion where Eric writes to Edward about his (Eric's) conversion to catholicism, it is stressed that it is to be kept a secret from the family. Everywhere in the society and the relationships of the novel there is duplicity, deceit and reserve, where people's lives are a trail of wreckage after the war. Isherwood is displaying the vanities that are preventing significant action and the fulfilment of the self in life. The failure to live and the inability to find the courage to break free of the past and of unacceptable values are the real subjects of the book.

Both novels approach self-analysis through wider social comment, but *The Memorial* is far more profound and more indicative of the lessons in self-knowledge that the age and the *Weltanschauung* appear to have required. Isherwood responded to the challenge by showing the same limbo as T. S. Eliot in (say) *The Hollow Men* or in the passages of *The Waste Land* that deal with the city, but Isherwood's people have a 'local habitation and a name' that make it possible for him to write a novel with levels of meaning. It is therefore rich in material for a reader wanting to understand the feelings and dissensions of the twenties writers who had missed the chance of The Test and who looked for alternative justifications and directions.

3

The Berlin Fiction and Documentary Writing of the 1930s

In his first two novels Isherwood had kept very close to his own biography and had used this material as a basis for exploring questions of moral identity and crisis for his contemporaries. In *Lions and Shadows* he wrote an autobiography that he stated should be read as a novel. This blurring of the distinction between the novel, autobiography and reportage was characteristic of the time, and was to become one of the most creative and innovative developments in the structure and scope of the novel throughout the thirties. Part of the impetus for this was, of course, the demand for factual information about foreign or sub-culture lifestyles. There was a new reading public which had literary and journalistic taste; there was a deep interest in films, and particularly in documentary films of working-class life. The rise of Fascism and Communism added to this fascination with other ways of living and organizing communities than the traditional English way. The restless generation of young people of Isherwood's age wanted to travel and to read about travels. The decade brought about new approaches to travel writing and this in turn had some influence on how the novel of social realism was to be written. Auden and Isherwood were commissioned to write a travel book at the end of the decade, *Journey to a War* (1938), but long before this Isherwood had understood and practised the art of mixing elements into one fictional framework: close observation, factual detail and informative dialogue would be his best tools for the task.

In 1949 Walter Allen looked back at these developments in the novel and attempted to explain them:

> So the characteristic prose of the thirties ... were works of
> autobiography like *A Georgian Boyhood* ... works of repor-
> tage like *Homage to Catalonia* and the various collections of
> mass observation reports. The novel was under a cloud, sus-
> pected of being frivolous unless it exposed the Means Test or
> demanded arms for Spain. The free play of imagination was
> verboten. The touchstone of a novelist's integrity was fidelity
> to his own immediate experience. More and more the setting
> of a novel became as contemporaneous as possible ....[1]

Clearly, this is a generalization and does not apply to all the
fiction of the time; moreover, Allen might have added that the
reportage and the autobiography helped other experimental
forms which include allegory, as in Rex Warner's *The Aerodrome* (1941). One might even see reportage as present in some
form in a work such as Waugh's *Decline and Fall* where a
satirical intention makes use of autobiographical conventions –
as is also found in Orwell's and Connolly's memoirs of school.
The implications of such developments in mixing genres are
what are most interesting in a reading of Isherwood.

Gareth Griffiths has interesting comments to make in relation
to these implications.[2] He notes that the autobiography and
reportage have increasingly been used by novelists in order to
find a means of defining identity. I think that this last point
explains what was unique to the genre that emerged in the thirties. Some novels were trying to define identity very overtly (a
genre that reached a point of intensity with the work of Denton
Welch) and others were trying to define society by means of
experience and what Auden called the 'intuitive glance'. We
have the Orwellian approach that takes a stereotype protagonist, such as Bowling in *Coming up for Air*, and by placing him in
contemporary society as an Everyman figure, turns fiction into
part-reportage by making their actions and experience symp-
toms of the malaise of the times. The more introverted writers
who used autobiography as a tool of fiction-reportage more
intensively, such as Walter Greenwood, James Hanley and
Isherwood, show a different intention. The difference can be
explained with reference to the naturalistic tendency of the
Orwellian type, which focuses on conventionality:

You know the road I live in – Ellesmere Road, West Bletchley?

Even if you don't, you know fifty others exactly like it. You
know how these streets fester all over the inner-outer suburbs.
Always the same. Long, long rows of little semi-detached
houses . . . .[3]

All fiction has to describe, but Orwell's is perhaps the most
typically didactic and factual of the period. The intention to
inform about hop-picking in Kent or parish life for a clergyman's
daughter is as firm as the objective of explaining characters'
motives and personalities.

Perhaps the best way to begin a study of Isherwood's place in
this hybrid genre is to look at his connection with John Lehmann's enterprising magazine, *New Writing*. His first two novels
had been intensely concerned with a series of personal crises,
though there had always been a vague awareness of proletarian
life. In both early novels he tries to introduce slight images of
this 'other England' – as in Philip's nocturnal adventures in London and in the cheap boarding-house or in Eric's links with the
miners. But his limitations in terms of first-hand experience of
areas of life outside his own privileged and comfortable existence had kept these things marginal in his writing. Naturally,
this precluded any sense of a comprehensive view with regard to
social trends or to the whole society. John Lehmann's approach
was eclectic but above all he wanted realism – no matter what
part of the world was reported on. He makes it clear that documentary writing was given special space and importance:

> In the same number was a section I had called 'Workers All', a
> symposium of short sketches and stories of the kind with
> which *New Writing* was perhaps most immediately associated
> in the mind of the public: stories of working-class life, of
> miners, factory-workers and the unemployed, on the border-
> line between fiction and reportage . . . .[4]

The element in the documentary novel that Isherwood found
suited his intentions was the scope it offered for being detached
from the material and avoiding sentimentality. Clearly, a great
deal of the writing in this genre at the time was sentimental in the
sense of being too concerned with personal reactions to social
injustice and with the effects of great social changes on the individual. The more experimental writing in the novel that was

beginning to attract Isherwood gave an added impetus to the techniques of depicting social realism. The documentary novel offered Isherwood opportunities to use his ideas of form and style, and these were not the same interests as those of many of his colleagues.

Therefore, to place Isherwood in the group of documentary realists of the thirties (with the Berlin books in mind) is to ask the question of how far these books, while showing another method of exploring personal identity, assume a didactic approach. One must also consider how this stance of the reportage/autobiographical novelist added to the force and success of the themes of identity that may be observed running through all his work.

The important distinction to make about Isherwood's writing as part of this trend of realism is that it is not proletarian writing in the sense that (say) B. L. Coombes' writing about South Wales miners' lives is. It is certainly not written by a worker or participant who writes from such an involved standpoint, yet neither are the Berlin books part of any special mission to report on the state of Germany under Nazism in the manner of some direct books of reportage of the time, such as Howard Smith's *Last Train from Berlin* (1938). It was quite by chance that the vogue for proletarian writing occurred at the time when Isherwood was preparing material for what were to become the one novel and related stories of the Berlin fiction, and there is no sound reason for suggesting that there was any force driving him to tell political truths in a journalistic way (there is an article written for *Action* magazine while he was living in the Nollendorfplatz but it is simply an objective and factual account of the Vandervogeln). The artistic intent and method in these books is just as serious and carefully developed from notebooks and diaries as is all his other fiction, as he has often said in interviews.

In *Christopher and his Kind* Isherwood makes a statement supporting the view that there was no overall aim in going to Berlin to study the working-class life there, or to carry on the autobiographical vein in a fresh setting. As stated on page 8, the motives were far less lofty. However, the place and people brought about significant advances in both his confidence as a person and in his expertise as a novelist. The Berlin fiction was 'documentary' in certain aspects only by chance – the natural outcome of experience and intuition. The diaries which were transformed into the fiction brought about a huge stride from the idea of familial and class identity to the study of the fundamental issue of how one understands oneself and reconciles selfish desire and vanity with the need to love and to understand others.

What explains the effect of Berlin on Isherwood's career is that there he escaped the literary life, and encountered at first hand the struggle for survival in ordinary life. Yet his motives for choosing Berlin were not entirely without an eye to finding artistic material in the atmosphere there. His discussion of the novel of epic proportions that was planned but never completed, *The Lost*, helps us here. The desire to make this work a social study as well as a kind of allegory developed gradually, and only in the writing of episodes that would form part of the grand design. In addition, there was a non-literary factor at work that had an effect on his writing: the psychology of Homer Lane, as propounded to W. H. Auden by John Layard (a disciple of Lane) before Isherwood went to Berlin. This theory was what the Isherwood of the earlier books had been searching for. It was a theory ideally suited to a writer who considered that one's notion of the self was created by the circumstances of family influence and social process. His warm reception of Lane's ideas explains a lot about the Berlin books and is especially illuminating with regard to the moral comment inherent in the actions of the characters of *The Memorial*. Lane's teaching is summarized in *Lions and Shadows*:

> Every disease, Lane had taught, is in itself a cure – if we know how to take it. There is only one sin: disobedience to the inner law of our own nature. The results of this disobedience show themselves in crime or in disease; but the disobedience is never, in the first place, our own fault. It is the fault of those who teach us, as children, to control God (our desires) instead of giving him room to grow.[5]

This is eccentric, dangerous and naive, but it is easy to see the strength of its appeal to the thirties generation. Also, as the close of *Lions and Shadows* makes clear, the move to Berlin was a desperate attempt to escape from his failures in England. These failures were, of course, all linked to family expectations.

Lane and Auden had made him realize the anarchic nature of his character: he was in search of a bohemian life. In view of the trivial and rather unambitious reasons for going to Berlin mentioned earlier (see pp. 8–9), it is not surprising that he did not find the writing of his great project easy at first. *The Lost* never developed, despite the fact that he had told Lehmann and E. M. Forster about it. The idea and the writing never suited his talents, as he reveals in *Christopher and his Kind*:

> He originally thought of this title in German, loving the solemn rolling sound of Die Verloren. He applied it to his subject matter with at least three separate meanings. It meant the 'doomed' – those who have lost their own way – that mass of Germans who were being herded blindly into the future by their Nazi shepherds. It meant those who, like Bernhard Landauer, were already marked down as Hitler's victims. And, in a lighter, ironic sense it meant ... moral outcasts.[6]

The Berlin stories that emerged are, in a sense, fragments of this over-ambitious, allegorical plan. However, Lehmann and Forster did see Isherwood as in some way a 'political' writer, and they also realized his individuality. In a letter to Lehmann, Forster laments the failure of the plan as if it promised something like the allegorical masterpiece that was to come from Malcolm Lowry later on. He referred to the need for a writer to chronicle the 'whole flux' and considered that something had been lost. Certainly, the main novel we have from that mass of material has elements that show that, given assistance and time, Isherwood had the potential to produce a panoramic novel that would cover the disparate features of life in Germany at the time.

If we move on now to the Berlin fiction itself, an examination of Isherwood's intentions will indicate the way that his artistic eclecticism led to a personal re-adaptation which is, it could be argued, only fully resolved in the best work of his American writing. The intention was to unite his own quest for self-knowledge with the documentary modes of the age: to report on the morality and values of that time and place from a liberal, cultured centre of consciousness. Mr Norris is himself a corruption of that stance, and so the satire and irony is much more potent.

The ability to understand Isherwood's scrutiny of the self

through fiction requires first a knowledge of his view of the conventional terms 'novel' and 'fiction'. It could be argued that fiction for him was important insofar as it may be autobiographical, moral and flexible in narrative method. Obviously, the problems of the 'Realism' of such forms have always been important, but his fiction is so embedded in subjectivity (often narcissism) that any attempt at objective reportage is quite arbitrary, despite the artistic success of the Berlin stories. To put it simply, the building up of scenes of sharp contrast, from social comment to autobiographical sequences, gives a structure of its own.

Isherwood's Berlin fiction is to be understood, perhaps, as allegory or parable, with the additional satirical comedy and modes of realism contained within the imaginative powers of the first-person narrator. The exploration of identity here is done by means of a compound creation of the narrator's character – a technique that has been used repeatedly since. The simple explanations of Isherwood's anonymity and complex use of 'camera eye', alter-ego and other discussions of self-dramatization, such as Alan Kennedy's, do not fully comprehend the depth of stylistic effect that is achieved in each book: Bradshaw, Chris, 'true' revelations of *Prater Violet* and so on. In a much more recent book, *Christopher and his Kind*, we find what purports to be a frank explanation of the use of 'I' in such multifarious ways. His concept of the remoteness of the writer's self of earlier years in relation to himself at present has been reinforced after a study of Vedanta and also from a reading of Erwin Schrodinger's book, *What is Life?* referred to in an interview of 1977:

> The youth that was I – you may never come to speak of him in the third person; indeed the protagonist of the novel you are reading is probably nearer to your heart, certainly more intensely alive and better known to you. Yet there has been no intermediate break, no death. And even if a skilled hypnotist succeeded in blotting out entirely all your earlier reminiscences you would not find that he had killed you.[7]

Isherwood, in many books and interviews, constantly emphasizes the importance to him of this distance from his earlier self – in each stage of development. It has also been far too easy to see in the Berlin fiction an obsession with recording 'the real truth', however trivial or self-concerned, and recording within this merely sensationalism and risqué sexuality. 'Herr Issyvoo' has been seen as narcissistic and the realism as journalistic concession to the 'New Writing' developments. Auden isolated such a trend in his 1930 journal when writing of autobiographical documentary, saying that realism was a form of anxiety neurosis, one of the many varieties of the jackdaw mind. 'One of the collectors against the reckoning day'. Narcissism enters in dealing with one's own experience and inferiority feeling in dealing with other people's, so Auden goes on to say. This attitude explains why the contemporary reviewers were ready to see political and documentary elements in fiction, whether intended or not. Realism was, in many instances in thirties writing, only a surface feature which informed about 'social conditions' and so on only with facts, lacking in creative perspectives.

The view that Isherwood's outstanding contribution to modern fiction has been in the thirties Berlin writings still persists, yet the nature of the narrator of the Berlin stories, it may be said, has not been fully appreciated. Samuel Hynes, for instance, expresses a common view, seeing Mr Norris as 'a conflict of public and private worlds'. Alan Wilde and Colin Wilson restrict discussion to stylistic matters and satire.

What I want to introduce here is the idea that the real prominence of the Berlin fiction lies in the exploration of identity, practised by a writer undergoing a rebellion from conventional family-centred morality; a novelist in a minority group, the homosexual, writing for the majority from which he dissents in terms of many moral values and taking as his subject a whole society and political-social system which showed in extremis the male power-dominated life which engulfed the tiny, artistic homosexual sub-culture at the time. Isherwood's fiction of the *New Writing* days during this time in Berlin, succeeded partly because he had learned the art of reportage within the novel, yet without writing that genre solely.

The standpoint of writing within a homosexual minority at the time was not quite the same as writing within a racial minority, but there are strong similarities in the sense of the uncertainties of feeling both significant and oddly unusual, worthy of scrutiny but also to be avoided. As Norman Mailer puts it: 'What charac-

terises the sensation of being a member of a minority group is
that one's emotions are forever locked in a chain of ambivalence'.[8] The ambivalence in Isherwood is one more example
of the rift between the man himself and the personae he presented and explored in locating the selves of his fiction. One
might speculate also that his mother's expectations of him and
his own earlier love of learning at school kept some vestigial
respect for the norms of English literary culture – things that are
part of the strength of Mr Norris's fictional success. In an interview with Robert Wennersten (1972) he hints at the importance
of this minority feeling: 'homosexuality has been used more as a
metaphor for belonging to a minority'. He also says that without
a minority viewpoint there is nothing to 'bounce off' and that he
needs always to see his fictional worlds with the eyes of a
stranger visiting a foreign land.

All this suggests that there was a dissent against something
closer to himself than even the violence of Nazism developing
and openly threatening innocent people around him in Berlin.
In the Bernhard section of his chapter 'The Landauers', in
Prater Violet and in Lions and Shadows there are many discussions of, and references to, English liberal culture, the one that
led to Isherwood's revolt from cosy family morality with its
narrowness and hypocrisy (as he saw it) and his self-imposed
exile. This is the source of much of the ambiguity of the narrator's standpoint – belonging and yet also part of a dissent. The
interpretations of England are always compounded with autobiographical reference and favourite stereotypes. In *Prater Violet* for instance, Bergmann is given this rich metaphor concerning umbrellas:

> You see, this umbrella of his I find extremely symbolic. It is
> the British respectability which thinks I have my traditions
> and they will protect me. Nothing unpleasant, nothing un-
> gentlemanly, can possibly happen to me within my private
> park.[9]

Bergmann is a father-figure to 'Isherwood' yet the book
exemplifies some of the most subtle indications of Isherwood's
awareness of the minority, homosexual standpoint as
Bergmann's teasing and lecturing about the English draws out
Isherwood's personal feelings. Bergmann understands the

'tragedy' of the Englishmen – they 'marry their mothers' – and he plans to write a novel called 'The Diary of an Etonian Oedipus' – but this stimulation of his protégé's mind grows to something more:

> Bergmann wanted all my time, all my company, all my attention. During those first weeks our working day steadily increased in length until I had to make a stand and insist on going home to supper. He seemed determined to possess me utterly. He pursued me with questions about my friends, my interests, my habits, my lovelife. The weekends especially, were the object of his endless, jealous curiosity. What did I do? Whom did I see? Did I live like a monk? 'Is it Mr W. H. you seek or the dark lady of the sonnets?' But I was equally obstinate. I wouldn't tell him. I teased him with smiles and hints.[10]

The scheme of *Prater Violet* confines the personal revelations of the Isherwood persona to his writings and political fears, up to the last few pages, where a voice of supposedly 'real' autobiography returns and something like an essay is interpolated. This is a general statement that looks back on the value of a life comitted to art and reflects on the nature of a personal view of homosexual love. In his love, there is 'The pain of hunger beneath everything. And the end of all love-making, the dreamless sleep after the orgasm, which is like death'.

The context of this statement is a confession of isolation and a fear of 'being afraid'. The book followed the main Berlin fiction, but to begin with *Prater Violet* establishes his personal position with regard to the 'love' that was an important part of the Berlin subject-matter: a thing that was full of the ambiguity that Mailer refers to. This uncertain ambiguity existed in fact and in the fiction, if we are to believe the end of *Prater Violet*. This is vital to the themes I am discussing because the fiction written in Berlin (or later writing about Berlin) is concerned largely with the various substitutes for healthy and proper human communication – part of which is conventionally labelled 'love'. The identity of the important narrator-character and the central figures is often ambiguous because of these themes, in addition to the doubt cast on the reader's judgements by the amoral subjects and the apparently nonchalant narrator.

There are always two contrasting worlds: in *Prater Violet* Isherwood has a 'home' and there is the studio where Bergmann is. In *Mr. Norris Changes Trains* there is Fraulein Schroeder's home and Norris's flat; even more definite, there is the division of 'visitor', 'teacher', 'confidant' and so on in Chris's relationships with Sally, Peter, Natalia, Bernhard and Frau Nowak in *Goodbye to Berlin*. Samuel Hynes sees this as especially important in *Mr. Norris Changes Trains* where a close personal relationship exists between Norris and Bradshaw long before the crime begins. The Bradshaw narrator is objective and also very much secondary in character-depth; he is also a depiction of the homosexual from within the atmosphere of British restrictive morality – the one that kept Forster's *Maurice* out of print and brought prosecution for James Hanley's *Boy* (1931) – and this narrator is faced with a new liberation in what Edgar Mowrer at the time called 'the freest republic in the world'. Mowrer cites the most popular literature of Kultur Bolshevismus of the thirties, fourteen titles from one shop-window in Berlin which included 'Flagellantism and Jesuit confessions' and 'The Whip in Sexuality', thus placing the context of Norris's perversions as quite credible – not mere exaggeration.

The narrator is infatuated by an ego that submits to this homosexual morality and lifestyle without guilt or pretence. More than this, Norris is a man who has amalgamated his perversion into society, even though this is part of a more general self of vanity and egocentricity which is exhibited in the Communist Party speech and in his frequent desire to dominate the weak. He is the homosexual who, unlike Isherwood or Bradshaw, has placed his identity in recognizable form in society – that is, he observes his own role-play and self-dramatization. The question of self-identity here is thus one that is answered by reference to a sub-culture within a culture, where a different morality may exist, autonomously. But the homosexual of Norris's type must exist in the main culture by means of a strained role-play – purely for survival (as recounted in Quentin Crisp's writings). The psychologist Ruitenbeek expresses the dilemma well:

> ... Contemporary homosexuality must be studied in a context other than that of mere sexual pathology. It is part of a larger, existential problem. The homosexual, like every other

person, must be aware of his behaviour; he must learn to be concerned less with the origin of his problem and more with how he deals with that problem. Does he accept himself for what he is and go on to experience more 'complete being in the world' or does he compulsively project his own inclinations on to others? Can he, in other words, be a person first and a homosexual second?[11]

Norris and the Isherwood surrogates in the stories exemplify these two types. Norris is the one who 'compulsively projects' his inclinations and Bradshaw is the first type, seeking full acceptance. Norris, the second type, is insecure when reality in any wider human context faces him. His complete self-delusion gives him a defence against weakness and doubt – which do affect Bradshaw. This contrast, surprisingly, does not dominate the Berlin fiction. The universal interest in identity displaces this, as Kennedy suggests:

> The wistful desire to belong to an ordered and hierarchical society never becomes more than a vague dream. So troubled are they with the problems of their own inescapable individuality that at times any relief seems appealing.[12]

Norris has examined the 'ordered and hierarchical society' of his earlier life and rejected it.

Mr. Norris Changes Trains best exemplifies the combination of the moral exploration of identity with the documentary manner of the time. The really ironic element in Norris is that his role-play consists of the image of the culture he has rejected: the public school gentleman. One qualification must be added here, however, and that is the fact that the element of rebellion and subversion in Isherwood's attitudes to conventional morality, so prominent in the autobiographical books, is not needed in the mode of writing used in Mr Norris's story. The true rebellion that led to the subject matter of the Berlin fiction is indicated in *Kathleen and Frank*:

> And what kind of father would Frank have been in his fifties if he had survived to become a brigadier-general and the Commandant of Kneller Hall? He might have tried hard to understand Christopher as a young man of the Freudian twenties

... at best they might have agreed to differ like gentlemen, after Christopher had wasted precious years of youth-time breaking the dreadful news slowly to Frank about boy-love ....[13]

In the fiction this cause of rebellion is conspicuous by its absence, if the reader expects it to be an overt criticism of the past generation, but it is nevertheless there. Norris is a member of Bradshaw's father's generation who does understand and appreciate boy-love and in addition, he is openly critical of the values and traditions that Kathleen and Frank lived by. Norris is uprooted from the English liberal culture of his youth, but the vestiges of this within him are a major part of his charm and his success – as well as of his corruption. When he and Bradshaw meet in the first chapter, Bradshaw comments:

I was now quite resigned to playing the relationships game. It was boring but exacting and could be continued for hours. Already I saw a whole chain of easy moves ahead of me – uncles, aunts, cousins, their marriages and their properties.[14]

However, Norris does not want to play this 'game'. He is outside the mores of that class (as is Bergmann) and also outside the sexual orthodoxy which is the foundation of that moral order.

The scheme of characterization, presenting Norris as a liar and deceiver, living on the surface of reality and pursued by the sinister Schmidt, gives Isherwood a fiction that mirrors the real with the evilly deceptive. This functions on two levels: Norris relates to the Communist Party and to all his peers with the same lack of adherence and comprehension that Bradshaw relates to the political and social norms of Berlin and the growth of Nazism. In other words, the novel divorces its 'reality' from its people, and this reflects the separation of Norris's self from its physical, role-playing animal mechanism – the level on which he works as a sheer embodiment of corruption.

Norris adjusts to material circumstances without allowing seriousness to impinge on him. His reactions are puerile in a laboured way:

And here we are, riding in the lap of luxury. The social reformers would condemn us, no doubt. All the same, I suppose if somebody didn't use this dining car we should have all these employees on the dole as well. . . . Dear me, dear me. These things are so complex these days.[15]

He is at once a commentator on capitalism and on his own need for self-justification. Repeatedly throughout the novel he justifies actions of habit and routine by means of an apothegm, and his witty generalizations owe a lot to the Oscar Wilde tradition: 'The German official all over ... a race of non-commissioned officers' and 'I can truthfully say that for sheer stupidity and obstructiveness, I have never met anyone to equal the small Berlin tradesman' are examples that maintain his prejudices while adding to our impression of his overall superficiality.

Norris's petty ritual supports his self-deceptive role and his escape from having to know himself. His jokes, Bradshaw observes, are part of this, and also his minute attention to appearance and fastidious attitude to food. His deception even extends to creating an elaborate myth of his true profession when he lies to Bradshaw. The complex account of his business in Chapter 2 shows this well.

The Troika cabaret shows the emergence of Bradshaw's identity as proselyte and Boswell to Norris. He is drunk and takes in even the lowest immorality as a simple pleasure; the beating up of Norris is a flagellation by Anni and it is significant in a deeper sense that Bradshaw mistakes pleasure for suffering. It is perhaps one of the most successful attempts to give the reader a metaphorical insight into the nature of his expatriots in the land of incomprehensible fascination and revulsion. Norris himself refuses to allow the full reality of his pleasure in flagellation. When Helen refers to the whores 'who dress up to excite the boot-fetichists' Norris replies:

'Well, upon my soul, ha ha I must say'. Arthur sniggered, coughed and rapidly fingered his wig, 'Seldom have I seen such an extremely, if you'll allow me to say so, er, advanced, or shall I say modern young lady.'[16]

His self-dramatization here is, as always, his protection from the full penetration of reality and its discomforts into his sensibility. Also, his self-myth creates a different person at every meeting with Bradshaw. Perhaps the most informative description here is of Norris as 'One of the last of the gentlemanly adventurers ... generally at my best in the witness-box'.

Until Schmidt is further developed, it seems that Norris is in the independent adventurer tradition, surviving by wit and by talent to deceive, yet later it becomes clear that he is possessed by Schmidt, who becomes symbolic of the detached possession of Norris's social self by a controlling self. He is the employee who 'owns' the employer. Schmidt controlled and doled out Arthur's pocket-money Bradshaw admits. It is only fitting that Arthur should be dogged by Schmidt to every part of the world, as Norris's existence is parasitic and dependant; one could speculate on the name Schmidt – or Smith – the common man whom he preys upon, becoming symbolic of nemesis. His own social role-play self is his ruin. He is at the mercy of a manifested other self of his own creation.

The links with Bayer and Heinz in the plot, of course, are essential for the reportage episodes. Once more, Norris, although seen by the Communist workers as a great orator and supporter of the proletariat, is not a participant. He cannot find identity in belief or in action as he is a study of the uncommitted individual, the unattached self. He says that he merely sympath-izes with the attitude of the German Communist Party.

Because Norris is so outstandingly a man who avoids facing the reality of his self, he is clearly an illustration of how Isher-wood's plan for *The Lost* could have worked out in a profound way. His involvement with Bayer particularly adds to the depths of the novel as a political exploration, using comic irony to express contemporary comment, as in the lecture scene:

> A slight stir, as if of uneasiness, passed over the rows of listeners. But the pale, serious, upturned faces were not ironic. They accepted without question this urbane, bourgeois gentleman, accepted his stylish clothes, his graceful rentier wit. He had come to help them. Bayer had spoken for him. He was their friend.[17]

The entire description is extremely sympathetic to the ordinary German proletariat, yet the presence of Norris is absurdly farcical in the serious political context.

With the technique of using Norris in this way, a portrait of a purely hedonistic self appears. The element in the fiction that may be labelled journalistic or documentary is relegated to direct statement – as opposed to the complexity of Norris's ironical position vis-à-vis the themes described by Isherwood in his outline of *The Lost*. The very purposeful 'background' scenes do serve a useful function, however, in showing the contrast of outer, public corruption and evil compared with Norris's private, individual corruption. The location and evocation of the truth of Nazi Berlin are intrinsic to Isherwood's purpose: the accounts of attacks on ordinary citizens for instance, with references to deathbed photographs of heroes and martyrs killed in street brawls. The significance of this looseness of form is that Norris moulds naturally into the construction of the other Berlin stories as yet another version of a 'lost' person, as detached from self-understanding as the wider society around him. He makes an excellent comparison with Bergmann in that Bergmann forces the weight of reality upon himself, shouldering emotional burdens; Norris simply presents an image. He is the most extreme lost soul in a moral emptiness, a limbo where truth is not the object of any quest or objective. As T. S. Eliot said,

Hell is alone, the other figures in it merely projections. There is nothing to escape from and nothing to escape to. One is always alone.

This escape from the knowledge of the self has been studied by theologians such as Martin Buber, who talks of 'reflexion':

I term it reflexion when a man withdraws from accepting with his essential being another person in his particularity – a particularity which is by no means to be circumscribed by the circle of his own self.[18]

Isherwood has described such a self in Norris – a man of surface gestures and actions that often forms well-worn stereotypes in fiction, but here the fictional characteristics have concentrated on satirical and moral comment which goes deeper than some accepted views of this Berlin writing.

The aspect of rebellion is also important here. Repeatedly, Isherwood uses Norris as the figure of a rebel who is a rebel through utter selfishness. Isherwood often refers to his own

dissent from the morality of family and culture that produced
Victor Page types, but even more ubiquitous and deeply felt is
the revolt discussed earlier against the heterosexual norm. The
consequent ambiguous moral standpoints owe much to this revolt. Isherwood adds D. H. Lawrence to Lane in attempting to
explain himself in this context. He discusses 'right' and 'wrong'
feelings for instance, and the idea of self-sacrifice. Of course,
Isherwood was partly attracted to their teachings because of the
seeming justification of his abandonment of his familial identity,
yet, especially if one also brings Lawrence's essay on pornogra-
phy and *Jane Eyre* to mind, one sees that these teachings on
morality apply as much to art as life, and Isherwood took his art
very seriously. It was clearly important to him that in writing
about the rebellion of a minority, truth must be adhered to.

   A great deal of *Mr. Norris Changes Trains* is concerned with
the interdependence common to all classes and occupations
within the homosexual fraternity of the Troika and even of the
Communist Party and the mysterious Margot for whom Norris is
illicitly working. The 'liberation' of all these groups is not
merely their freedom of sexual activity, but their freedom to
submit to the restraints of minority life and the problems of an
alternative morality. When Isherwood summed up his feelings
on Norris later, he had this to say:

> What repels me now about *Mr. Norris* is its heartlessness. It is
> a heartless fairy story about a real city in which human beings
> were suffering the miseries of political violence and near-star-
> vation. The 'wickedness' of Berlin's nightlife was of a most
> pitiful kind; the kisses and embraces, as always, had price-tags
> attached to them, but here the prices were drastically reduced
> in the cut-throat competition . . . .[19]

The teachings of Lane and Lawrence clearly would apply to an
amoral society – whether amoral in comparison to the British
morality he knew or in the Berlin demi-monde sense where, for
the sake of the novel, Isherwood refused to take any open moral
stance. The 'right' kind of feelings invented by professional
moralists and the resulting self-sacrifice had their counterpart in
the kind of freedom (enjoyed by Sally, Norris, Bernhard and
Otto) which was the prison of Buber's reflexion. Nevertheless,
sexuality is central to the relationships described in the Berlin

fiction, and this contractual, economic nexus of human relationships represents for Isherwood (as for Lawrence) the supremely immoral nature of man when set against norms of morality at a particular historical moment. When the historical moment happens to be the rise of Nazi fascism and the genesis of a world war, the individual morality is all the more meaningful. Isherwood shows that the novel is the genre that can best accommodate this artistic impulse.

I see the value of *Mr. Norris* and of the short stories (the latter not being in the scope of this study) as being an exploration in vivid, visualized and documentary, of a world without agreed moral order, where each character is in a selfless world of non-knowledge and untruth, existing without even the ability to search for self-knowledge. There is a moment in the story of 'The Nowaks' in *Goodbye to Berlin* which reveals this particularly well. Bradshaw is observing the Nowak family, where Frau Nowak and Otto are the two polarities of commitment to morality and revolt respectively, and Bradshaw describes the fiction he is currently writing:

> It was about a family who lived in a large country house on unearned incomes and were very unhappy. They spent their time explaining to each other why they couldn't enjoy their lives; and some of the reasons were most ingenious.[20]

The full force of this is only understood in context; the narrator is living in physical contact with the people of a minority – sexual or economic – and sees their anger and revolt as understandable yet futile. In ironic contrast, the highest representatives of his English liberal culture and the orthodox morality he knows do not understand either their motivations or their desires. However, the latter group are in Bradshaw's mind; they form a worrying contrast with the immediate 'amoral' world he lives in, with Otto at its centre. Once again, the implication is that lack of self-knowledge is the basic and universal human problem.

To summarize these strands of thought would be helpful here. Isherwood chose to depict an amoral context in which the many modes of exploring or denying self exist in a group of characters, with Norris as the focal point. This matches what we know of the hypothetical *The Lost* as he describes its conception: 'The link between which binds all the chief characters together is that in some way each of them is conscious of the mental, economic and ideological bankruptcy of the world in which they live.

The fragmentary form in which we have the work – one novel and a group of stories – is changed in shape and in scope. As Isherwood admitted in an interview, the protagonists are much more deeply studied and the reportage sequences add an effective contrast to the individual experience centred on Norris and Bradshaw in the novel (and on the narrator's relationships with Sally, Bernhard and Otto, particularly in the stories).

Finally, the autobiographical element in the Berlin fiction is found to be much less significant when seen in this way. The persona of the writer has at last escaped his bedrock in Isherwood's increasingly solipsistic attitudes to fiction. Consequently, the documentary novel appears a very different thing in Isherwood's hands from what was the norm in the genre. In fact, this casts doubt on critical attempts to put uniformity on the genre that dominated thirties fiction. G. S. Fraser has suggested such a doubt and he too saw Isherwood as somehow individual:

> I worry a little about the documentary novel. It was a real concept in the thirties, connected with the high achievements of the British documentary film. The idea behind it was that detached, cinematic observation of carefully chosen episodes would bring out social significance, not imposed by the novelist. The trouble is that the only really distinguished practitioner one can think of now is Christopher Isherwood.[21]

Fraser seems to be separating Isherwood from novelists such as James Hanley and Walter Greenwood, and he does this because of the point about structure. This makes sense, and it is hoped that my study has isolated a writer who was merely using a current genre for his own artistic purposes. If the novel and stories that came from the Berlin experience were merely classified 'faction', to use the modern term, then the themes present in the writing which I have discussed would be reduced in significance. Isherwood's own phrase, 'a fairy story', is closer than he thinks, for the mode of writing often detracts from the orthodox realism, thus creating the individuality of Isherwood's approach.

4
The Berlin Period: Shorter Fiction

The fiction that Isherwood produced in the thirties, while in Berlin, has been judged in reappraisals and reviews as his best work because it shows a society in upheaval and decadence, illustrating a period of history that turned out to be of great significance. In addition, this writing evinces a descriptive and visual power which compares with that of Orwell or Greene in their most successful political novels of the thirties and forties. The contemporary response was one that saw the same immediacy and relevance in his fiction that could be observed in the Left Book Club publications (1934 onwards) and even before this, in Orwell's *Down and Out in Paris and London*. Samuel Hynes cites a review by William Plomer which saw in *Mr. Norris Changes Trains* 'A parable of the modern historical situation'. Plomer says this of the Communist Party element in the book:

> ... it may be taken as a comment on the state of civilisation in general during these last few years, and it may be that in Ludwig Bayer, a Communist leader, we are tentatively to anticipate the possibility of a cleaner and better behaved world.[1]

As Hynes says, Isherwood doubted the accuracy of this reading, but since he contented himself with recording behaviour and although he 'was quite aware that this material was material',[2] the seriousness of Bayer's behaviour compared with the dilettante narcissism of Norris, and Bayer's ultimate ruin, make the 'parable' that Plomer read into it quite valid.

The genre of the novel in the thirties was not perhaps seen as the best vehicle for parable (the plays of Auden and Isherwood

49

are bolder attempts); yet in the novel also allegorical approaches to political themes were developed in Rex Warner's *The Professor* and *The Aerodrome*. I prefer to use the term 'parable' here rather than allegory, as allegory implies (from usage in general) a more consistent and deliberately patterned structure. My use of parable as a term is simply intended to show that moral intentions may be detected in a plot and characters where their representative nature, not necessarily just as social stereotypes, is easily noted.

For parable to be seen as a valid and viable form by contemporaries, it had to mix with the recent conventions of socio-realism. Orwell may be seen as a precursor of this type of writing; in *Burmese Days*, where Imperialism is his butt, he uses Flory as a kind of representative figure in a parable which expresses anti-Imperial dissent. The documentary approach of the socio-realists of the Left Book Club and Mass Observation was always open to the use of such moral parable, despite the fact that imagination was secondary to fact. Isherwood's original intention, I would suggest, was to keep firmly to moral questions about action and identity. The reason for his use of parable is that the intention was partly subconscious. He was not trying to overemphasize or present a casebook. Nevertheless, his Berlin fiction matches Auden's explanation of the force of parable in art:

> You cannot tell people what to do, you can only tell them parables; and that is what art really is, particular stories of particular people and experiences, from which each may draw his own conclusions.[3]

This feature emerges in the Berlin fiction as Isherwood's intention to pinpoint moral values becomes apparent. Isherwood's wish to use personal extensions of a semi-autobiographical nature prevent this allegorical development. The characters themselves, however, are representative as well as particular. Isherwood has said that character creation is 'a magical process of thinking of them in their eternal, magic, symbolic aspects'.[4] Frl. Schroeder, Otto, Herr Landauer, Wilkinson, Bergmann, Bowles and even Norris, have a great deal of the stereotype in their make-up, as they are part of the scheme of representative isolation that was Isherwood's aim behind the projected 'epic', *The Lost*.

Before looking at the allegorical and moral elements here, some account of the genesis of the form of the books must be given. An illuminating account of the emergence of *New Writing* occurs in John Lehmann's recent *Thrown to the Woolfs* (1981) where he recalls that Isherwood and he expressed a wish to see an equivalent of the French *roman* in English literature, where structure did not have to match a conventional vastness of scope. *New Writing* was not quite able to encourage this form, but the sections of *Goodbye to Berlin* show how much the kind of miniature picaresque where adventures relate closely to character suited Isherwood. The actions in this *roman* type are created more to reveal character or abstract concept than to develop plot. This approach is suitable for a fiction where anecdote, digression and supposed autobiography mix. *The Lost* was never written, mainly because Isherwood was writing three books at once and didn't have time to complete all of them (see the letters quoted by Lehmann). He was, partly because of Lehmann, seeing his writing as socio-realism rather than as a purely imaginative and impressionistic interpretation of his era:

> ... it is written entirely in the form of a diary without any
> break in the narrative. It will have lots of characters and be full
> of 'news' about Berlin. Frank journalism, in fact.[5]

His confusion about which book – or which mode – to develop is emphasized when, by 1934, he had completed *Mr. Norris Changes Trains*. Shortly after this he was adapting his fragments of *The Lost* for use in *New Writing*:

> A month later a postcard arrived: 'The Kulaks are coming.
> Hope you'll like them'. This was the original name for the first
> of the long-short stories he had worked up out of what re-
> mained of *The Lost*, after Mr Norris had been given an in-
> dependent life.[6]

As this organization of various sections of *The Lost* continued, Isherwood showed a preference for the personal diary type of writing and found weaknesses in *Sally Bowles*. However, the final book form of *Goodbye to Berlin* presents enough material to form an impression of the scheme behind the abandoned epic.

The fragmentary and digressive writing suits the material
well, as the opening and closing diary sections enclose the writing within the traditional intimate *Bildungsroman* atmosphere
of the young man's experiences. The diary element also pinpoints the Isherwood persona's moral stance. It is clear that he is
an innocent eye immersed in a 'destructive element':

> One day I asked Frl. Schroeder straight out: what was Frl.
> Kost's profession? 'Ha ha, that's good! That's just the word
> for it. Oh yes, she's got a profession. Like this – And with the
> air of doing something extremely comic, she began waddling
> across the kitchen like a duck, mincingly holding a duster
> between her finger and thumb. Just by the door, she twirled
> triumphantly round, flourishing the duster as if it were a silk
> handkerchief, and kissed her hand to me mockingly. 'Ja ja,
> Herr Issyvoo! That's how they do it!' 'I don't quite under-
> stand Frl. Schroeder. Do you mean she's a tightrope
> walker?'[7]

It is important, if a moral parable is to function by contrast, that
Isherwood must be outside his subject matter although he 'lives'
within it and participates, in the manner of Conrad's Marlow.
Thus his naivety is shown here perhaps too obviously. Similarly,
his affection for Sally, Otto and Bernhard must be indulgent and
omit to point out real evils as opposed to peccadilloes, they are
for the reader to judge. The didactic element must be omitted
from the fictional parable that grows steadily. Each story has its
effect on the narrator's innocence and each series of characters
within each story has one outstanding example of a lostness – as
Isherwood explained his design in letters to Lehmann. Sally is
lost in her amorality of self-delusion; Peter is lost in the mental
turmoil of possession and jealousy; Otto and the Nowaks are
Germany in terms of ordinary people – those lost in a welter of
circumstances and groping their way in ignorance. The three
main characters share a different, abnormal and cruel attitude to
love and human relationships. Sally is the hetaira, restricting
sexuality to commerce; Peter is the parasite on the goodness of
Frau Nowak, and Bernhard is the final outcome of inhumanity –
he is 'lost' to others and to himself.

The educative experience for the reader comes through the
narrator, but not through the narrator's eyes. The narrator must

be amoral and distant; he is locked in objectivity and can only record for us; he does not register the expected reactions of indignation or pity, but we can.

In addition, there is a parallelism in the corruptions presented: Sally is a human failure whereas Peter and Bernhard have their failures rooted firmly in social causes. Sally fails through a hard ambition and the temptation to give all for a dream: Peter, especially, dominates others, as Germany seemed to be doing at the time.

I hope to show that the conclusion is that the causes of evil and inhumanity are to be found in aspects of the self that adhere too closely to possession and control. The parable has most force in the emotional tragicomedy of Frau Nowak. Parable here is used in the sense of a highly moral commentary working by implication. The actions of protagonists are to be judged on one level as outcomes of background, family and circumstances; on another as undesirable and inhuman products of an era with a specific nature which may be encompassed by parables as much as facts.

Sally Bowles illustrates these features well. There is detailed explanation of her family background, and she is a stereotype in some ways of a dilettante, 'county' type, complete with allowance and inheriting a certain priggery; yet we know that her promiscuity is a form of life she leads without an affectional motive: sensuality and ambition are her motives. Her self-delusion is her lostness in the demi-monde of the Lady Windermere Cabaret. The lies about her mother being French, her excuses for her hatreds and above all her reasons for her abortion, expose an empty, deluded and meaningless life. Her lostness, in the end, derives from her particular comprehension of reality. She does not judge experience, but treats experience as unimportant. The central plot of her affair with Kurt and the abortion illustrates this well. She 'loves' him but when he has left her she considers only the financial loss and when her pregnancy has to be fully realized, she keeps the reality at a distance by self-dramatization: she has her reasons well prepared:

'Will the doctor . . .?'
'No, he won't.' I asked him straight out. He was terribly shocked. I said: 'My dear man, what do you imagine would happen to the unfortunate child if it was born? Do I look as if I'd make a good mother?'[8]

The full effect of this is only felt when the context of Clive's (the American's) brand of lostness is considered. Sally 'adores' him immediately and helps in his search for the 'real'. Clive was lost in uncertainty as to the validity of reality also:

> Was this the genuine article? Was this the guaranteed height of a real GOOD TIME? It was? Yes, yes of course – it was marvellous![9]

Sally is drawn to other hedonists who support her surface apprehensions of reality and who, in R. D. Laing's terminology, 'collude' with her personal myth of her identity as something she is not. Sally exists for sensual pleasure which is never recognized as transitory and only her own obsession with self is 'reality' for her. Her self is the only means of comprehending life-data, and is therefore very selective in what it allows through into her own emotions. At the funeral of Herman Muller there is this indication of her relation to political-social reality as the documentary novel would have it:

> 'Say, who was this guy anyway?' asked Clive, looking down. 'I guess he must have been a big swell?'
> 'God knows,' Sally answered, yawning. 'Look Clive darling, isn't it a marvellous sunset?'[10]

This scene is crucial to the counterbalance between narrator and characters, as 'Christopher' identifies with her hedonist outlook and sees her comment as merely a hint that the political world means nothing to them:

> Perhaps in the Middle Ages people felt like this, when they believed themselves to have sold their souls to the devil. It was a curious, exhilarating and not unpleasant experience; but, at the same time, I felt slightly scared. Yes, I said to myself, 'I've done it now. I am lost.'[11]

'Isherwood' believes that he has left the comprehensible world of subjective reality – that of Frl. Schroeder, the world from which he ventures as investigator and recorder. As Schroeder's reality is human in its constant comedy, purposeless business is happily recognized to be so and the necessities and duties of life keep the comprehension of reality healthy and innocent in contrast to the Berlin outside. Sally makes a false, pretended concession to conventional morality in the hospital, as the most deluded expression of her alienation from self-knowledge; she has given Christopher's name as her husband and created a false picture of herself. Yet only a short time before this the doctor's costs had been reduced in order that Sally could buy some new night-dresses.

Finally, her ultimate statement of separation from true perception of her place in her social milieu comes when she dramatizes the reaction to the abortion and her 'maternal longings':

> I don't know ... I feel as though I'd lost faith in men. I just haven't any use for them at all. ... Even you, Christopher, if you were to go out into the street now and be run over by a taxi ... I should be sorry in a way of course but I shouldn't really care a damn.[12]

There are two areas of experience in the stories: one where this knowledge of reality, or involvement with it, fails people, and one where the knowledge of others fails them. Sally and Peter Wilkinson want to avoid all effort towards self-understanding and sympathy for others. The Isherwood narrator, to isolate the complex nature of his persona, shares this unwillingness to be known by others:

> I had tried to compete with her beastly little Kurt on his own ground; just the very thing, of course, which Sally had wanted and expected me to do! After all these months I had made one fatal mistake – I had let her see that I was not only incompetent but jealous. I could have kicked myself. The mere thought made me prickly with shame from head to foot.[13]

In this way the narrator perceives his seduction away from independence. In the end, the degree of self-knowledge is the measure of success in this world, and each sees – even dramatizes – his or her drifting away from this knowledge.

The other parable in *Goodbye to Berlin* is the one of the self lost without the capacity to love or without relationships in a capitalist society where one is a kind of commodity. Otto Nowak and his family exemplify this lostness within a social system. Where Sally had self-dependence through ignorance of the claims of morality, the Nowaks lose independence gradually through the close awareness of the reality forced upon them by the impersonal forces of history and economics. They are also 'lost' in the sense that their being more fully human makes them weaker and exploitable. Frau Nowak is thus assigned the representative tragic role of her class in this particular historical context. Her story is one of dignity and self-esteem where the parable, in contrast to Sally's, has a more noble kind of self-delusion, but this exists only beneath her immersion in hard reality:

> Then, the flat's so damp at this time of year. You see those marks on the ceiling? There's days we have to put a footbath under them to catch the drips. Of course, they've no right to let these attics at all really. The inspector's condemned them time and time again. But what are you to do? One must live somewhere.[14]

However, even within this atmosphere there is another lost man: Otto. In an amoral world, Otto lives the commercial and possessive relationships like Sally. The difference is that Otto has the animal instinct to be aware of what the forces of economics and of political ideology may do to him and his kind. He quarrels violently with his mother but at least has pity for her. His animal nature is haunted by the irrational because he cannot impose his ego on life. For instance, Isherwood uses the account of his nightmare to hint at his fears, where he describes seeing 'a great black hand stretching over the bed ...'. He dramatizes experience, as Sally does, often in a type of dumb show; and his communication relies on physical gesture and expression: 'a dry, monkey-like leer of malice' and so on. He is a tormentor and a clown. Further, he is always shown as being outside the otherwise close family and even his suicide attempt indicates that he will go to any extreme to win possession of another person; even on being consoled by Christopher, Otto ends his apparent despair with words that show that self-dramatization is all we have seen: 'Why, Christoph ... this is one of mine!' he says, when a handkerchief catches his attention.

Isherwood's sombre vision, part nightmare and part conscious perception, of the 'Lost' isolated and doomed Nowaks gives us an insight into the nature of the lives of the Berlin proletariat behind the veneer of Nazi ideology. This is vividly evoked in the final paragraph of *The Nowaks* where Isherwood describes the people in the sanatorium where Frau Nowak is dying:

> They all thronged round us for a moment in the little circle of light from the parting bus, their lit faces ghastly like ghosts against the black stems of the pines. This was the climax of my dream: the instant nightmare in which it would end. I had an absurd pang of fear that they would attack us – clawing us from our seats, dragging us hungrily down in dead silence . . .[15]

The exits from the safe world of Frl. Schroeder have led almost to the crisis of his own destruction in a hedonist subculture. Only in the rooms there is Isherwood safely supported by the cosy womb of convention where he is 'Herr Issyvoo', almost a parody of the genteel, polite Englishman, punctual with his rent and openly respectable.

The reversion to 'pure journalism in fact' in the closing *Berlin Diary* completes the encapsulation of *The Lost* within their milieu. The diary recounts straightforward political attitudes and factual reportage, but the powerful close of the account of the German people themselves is told in the visit to the boys' reformatory. The moral of these parables of lost selves is reinforced by the explanation of the desire for freedom: the doors of the reformatory are always open but few leave. Christopher asks why this is so and is told, 'The system helps them to lose their desire for freedom. I think, perhaps in Germans, the instinct is never very strong'.

The suggestion is that the Nowaks and their kind are held also by the strength of conformity and custom and the moral comment in this statement is far more convincing than any detailed discussion of individuals would be. The reformatory becomes an image of the setting of hedonist escape from self-understanding. The stereotypes of the conscientious mother, grim Prussian brother, ingenuous clownish father and so on in the Nowak family take on a new depth when viewed in the light of their representative nature in this context. The words of the title,

Goodbye to Berlin, may be seen as an echo of that ambiguity at the end of the book which is so ironical and paradoxical:

> They, and the people on the pavement, and the teacosy dome of the Nollendorfplatz station have an air of curious familiarity, of striking resemblance to something one remembers as normal and pleasant in the past – like a very good photograph. No, even now I can't altogether believe that any of this has really happened . . . .[16]

Once again, Isherwood preserves the distance between reality in the reportage and the 'evidence' of his persona – 'aware that his material WAS material' – and the truth may not be on the surface. This helps to explain why the morality in the stories is so shifting, constantly elusive and distant from the reader's viewpoint.

Herbert Marcuse, in his book, *Negations* (1964) has something to say that is relevant here. He distinguishes between 'personal' and 'contractual' relationships in hedonist groups. His dichotomy defines clearly the relationships in Isherwood's stories as far as the main characters are concerned. Marcuse's central insight is that normal boundaries or definitions of these differing bases of relationships are blurred in such groups. People within these, he argues, '. . . cannot sustain happiness precisely when they are what they are intended to be'. For Marcuse, hedonism substitutes contract for personal attachment and it also creates subjection and weakens personal autonomy. Otto, for instance, has contractual relationships where he has a commodity as any labourer in Marxist terms would have, and this is the contractual hedonism that we see at the centre of many episodes in the fiction. In all cases, the self is no more than a thinly-perceived entity that demands pleasure and diversions because these are the only comprehensible means of perceiving the world. For the hedonist, the self is the focus of the world because all it consists of is pleasurable response to objects and so on. As Marcuse says, they cannot sustain happiness.

I have tried to stress in this chapter the nature of the Berlin stories as a game of willpower, one self against another, with the Isherwood persona adding depth to the study of the morality of such a community. The potential of this writing is only really fulfilled, however, in the persona's succumbing to one of the 'lost' in some way. The narrator's relationship with Bernhard is the nearest thing to a submission by him to the force of this demand for 'uncompromising knowledge' that Marcuse says the hedonist ego demands of others. Bernhard attracts Christopher largely because of his sardonic detachment from others. He teases Christopher. The narrator has to be seduced by the strongest will among the group. Near the maturity of their relationship, Bernhard is trying to gain the uncompromising knowledge by seeing the narrator as a specimen of humanity to be analysed and understood. Bernhard is explaining Christopher's motivations to him when Christopher loses control:

'Bernhard, you're being fantastic!'
'Am I? Perhaps .... But I do not think so. Never mind. Since you wish to know, I will try to explain why I brought you here ... I wished to make an experiment.'
'An experiment? Upon me, do you mean?'
'No. An experiment upon myself. That is to say ... for ten years I have never spoken intimately, as I have spoken to you tonight, to any human soul ....'[17]

This conveys Christopher's alarm, but he can never give Bernhard uncompromising knowledge of himself. He is too normal – in the sociological sense – and he has to remain close to the reader's stance. The important thing is that their relationship remains to some degree contractual: Christopher receives favours in return for his admiration and company.

Thus, Sally, Otto and Peter each shows, in his or her own way, the possessive nature of the hedonistic self that Marcuse describes in terms of the gratification of the individual as a 'goal within an impoverished reality'. Happiness, for the hedonist, will always be subjective. Maybe this reading of the patterns within the Berlin stories not only clarifies the nature of the often praised 'decadent' features of this phase in Isherwood's writing, but also makes his development as a novelist of faith and doubt more understandable.

Of course, the idea of a 'parable' suggests something rhetorical and sometimes grotesquely comic, as in Herr Nowak's clowning, but if a parable, in the sense that it is used here, tells a moral tale without obvious didacticism, then the form used by Isherwood suits the material admirably, as the objectivity of his

Berliners' behaviour is all the more convincing when not emphasized in the way that stigmatized the German people in the popular mythology of the twenties, ever since Katherine Mansfield's *In a German Pension* (1911). Neither was Isherwood's initial plan of *The Lost* a desire to tell the whole truth about the rise of Hitler as far as he was able. It would be tempting to compare his detached attitude to a subject matter that is so subtly a moral scrutiny with Emile Zola's idea of Naturalism where the objects of his fictions are 'human animals, nothing more'.[18]

5
The Influence of Vedanta on the Novels

There have been many opinions voiced in the last decade concerning Isherwood's 'conversion' (a term he disliked) to Vedanta, notably by Finney and Fryer in their biographies. However, these have not attempted to unite the autobiographical evidence with the themes of his work since *Prater Violet* (1946). Many appraisals of his religious life have been prejudiced by the general reaction to his abandonment of Britain and his settlement in America at the beginning of World War II – perhaps the first satire on him being Evelyn Waugh's references to Parsnip and Pimpernel (Auden and Isherwood) in *Put Out More Flags*.

However, such attitudes have eclipsed the truth about the meaning of faith for Isherwood in his life and in his writings. It could be said that the influence of Vedanta on Isherwood is something that has not yet been fully assessed. The earlier chapters of this book have described various stances that Isherwood assumed in order to judge his own lack of any fixed moral certainty or of any confidence as to his concept of self-identity, all these being part of an attempt to assess himself as a product of his class and so on.

In his first two novels he tried to resolve the tension between the imaginary, subconscious world of his personal obsessions and the effort to depict a civilization in moral disintegration. In the Berlin fiction he extended the scope of the study to that of amoral escape from self-understanding. It is quite logical to find such a writer being drawn to a new and individual approach to the problem of self-knowledge. The important point here, however, is that his urge to self-knowledge was artistic as well as religious. This is the most fruitful starting-point here. In an interview with Stanley Poss he says:

61

More and more, writing is appearing to me as a kind of self-analysis, a finding out something about myself and about the past, and about what life is like as far as I'm concerned; who I am; who these people are; what it's all about. And this comes from a subconscious level to some extent.[1]

The critic's problem when he considers Vedanta as an influence on Isherwood's novels is to reconcile this with Isherwood's statement, made also in 1961, that 'I can't honestly say that Vedanta has had any effect on me as a writer. I don't see the world, or people, differently.[2] However, he does admit that 'it revealed to me the thing that lies behind the writing . . . in the religious life you try to see individuals sub specie aeternitatis'.[3] The impact of Gerald Heard, as described in Isherwood's essay in a memorial volume to Aldous Huxley and to Swami Prabhavananda was such that it caused a rebirth of interest in the scrutiny of man after the nihilism and defeat of the close of *Prater Violet*.

This closing section of *Prater Violet* is a useful reference here. Isherwood had, before the novel, emphasized conventional techniques of realism, particularly dramatic dialogue, and there was a growing sense of dissatisfaction with what he saw as a superficial and limited method. The narrator of *Prater Violet* witnesses the recession of social and moral identity at the end of a novel that has been, on one level, a study of the possession of a weak ego by a dominant one. He extends this theme of the inadequacy of man alone or man too weak to be alone:

It was that hour of the night at which man's ego almost sleeps. The sense of identity, of possession, of name and address, grows very faint. It was the hour at which man shivers, pulls up his coat collar and thinks: 'I'm a traveller, I have no home'.[4]

There is a suggestion that he was not entirely ignorant of the limitations of much conventional realism; he was beginning to perceive the value of the universal and eternal qualities of humanity and his past methods were inadequate. Realism as we now appreciate it, after Beckett and the influence of psychology on the novel, was something under the surface of pre-war documentary fiction. Psychological study of characters through their illogical and fragmented language was not then carried out to the extremes to which modern playwrights, for instance, have taken realistic technique. The importance of self-knowledge emerged from this, and it was never more cogently expressed in Isherwood's work than in the close of this novel:

> What was he thinking about? 'Prater Violet', his wife, his daughter, myself, Hitler, a poem he would write, his boyhood or tomorrow evening? How did it feel to be inside that sticky body, to look out of those dark, ancient eyes? How did it feel to be Friedrich Bergmann?[5]

The narrator simultaneously registers the dominating functions of the everyday awareness of self – a poor, mechanical thing. He becomes conscious of what Colin Wilson has called 'the robot self', meaning the narrower functions of the self that perform daily psychomotor skills and allow the 'mind' to be seemingly dormant – but in reality performing routine activities.

The remaining pages face up to that other factor in Isherwood's life: love. Yet the word denotes only the current homosexual affair:

> After J. there would be K and L and M, right down the alphabet. It's no use being sentimental. Because J isn't really what I want. J has only the value of being now. J will pass, the need will remain. The need to get back into the dark, into the bed, into the warm, naked embrace, where J is no more than J, than K or L or M .... The pain of hunger beneath everything.[6]

The unease with this form of love is casually contrasted with the brief assertion that he loved Bergmann and that the cause of this love had initially been their union of two private selves into the one self of 'artist' in the making of their film.

A close reading of this novel, then, indicates that Isherwood was beginning to see the limits of his former literary and moral perceptions. Self and others and love he had understood only shallowly, as he admits. He then intensified and deepened his literary and moral preoccupations throughout the work which followed this novel, and that the writing from *The World in the Evening* (1954) to *A Meeting by the River* (1967) is his most artistically successful as he carefully explored themes that are

universal and particularly contemporary. The division of man
from his gods and the self from its alliance with the flux of
sense-impressions of reality, and its relationship with the idea of
the other are what concerns him in this later fiction.

Twentieth-century literature has offered various explanations
of the separation of mankind from religious certainty. In many
ways, the most important precursor of Isherwood in this respect
could arguably be Herman Hesse, in his novel *Siddhartha* (1922)
especially. Isherwood, through his study of Hinduism has much
in common with Hesse, but their techniques are markedly
different, despite the closeness of their subject-matter. Both
have a string theme which explores the divorce from objective
reality and transcendence, but Hesse explains too directly; philosophy is inextricably mixed with the fiction: 'Time is not real
Govinda. I have realised this repeatedly. And if time is not real,
then the dividing-line between this world and eternity, between
suffering and bliss, between good and evil, is also an illusion'.[7]

This idea of attachment to place and time, vital to the philosophy of Vedanta, is much more subtly revealed in Isherwood,
although he still has to explain as he writes. The didactic was one
extreme option open to him when he began writing religious
novels; the Beckettian extreme was another. This also he rejected. For example, Beckett's *The Lost Ones* explores the sen-
sations of being-in-the-world that interest Isherwood but all
specific details of time and place are ignored:

> Abode where lost bodies roam each searching for its lost one.
> Vast enough for search to be in vain. Narrow enough for flight
> to be in vain. Inside a flattened cylinder fifty metres round and
> eighteen high for the sake of harmony. The light. Its dimness
> . . . . It is perhaps the end of their abode.[8]

Beckett here exemplifies the objectivity and alienation of the
world as the person most 'really' perceives it, in terms of the
attempt to communicate love and make relationships. Isherwood, however, cannot remove the social context of his account
of being-in-the-world, but he shows the same isolation of self
from the world by his fictional representations of the Hindu
concept of 'maya' – the unreality of ever-changing phenomena.

Beckett's use of the word 'abode' avoids any sense of spatial
or temporal context – which is what the Hindu view of reality

demands as part of the escape from self. But Beckett can only describe the undesirable kind of escape: despair and inertia. Attachment to time and place is bound firmly to moral sense. One cannot, according to Vedanta, have a moral involvement with the world without being bound to 'maya'. In Christian terms, God is the only judge.

Vedanta Hinduism sees life paradoxically as fluent yet apparently the same, therefore a judgement of life by man is one that must shift as life shifts. Such concepts changed Isherwood's view of life, and so changed his writing.

Isherwood chose in his religious novels a form, that has neither extreme – that of Hesse or of Beckett – in terms of style. Where Hesse tries to show a god being humanized, Isherwood sees the real impossibility of this within his kind of realism and so makes the style and content less didactic. Neither does he follow Beckett into fiction that leans too far into the solipsistic experience and omits the social experience as realistic fiction normally conceives it. When he first reflected on these religious novels, in interviews, he considered them as structural and theoretical problems concerned with a definite theme to be communicated from personal belief. In his essay, *The Problem of the Religious Novel*, he asks: 'How am I going to show in terms of dramatic fiction, that decisive moment at which my hero becomes aware of his vocation and decides to do something about it?'[9] He shows here the germ of his intention to concentrate on the problem of transferring religious ideas to literary form. Like all serious contemporary writers, he is aware of the recurrent preoccupation in existentialist writing – what Alan Swingewood sums up as 'alienation and reification' – and he adds that these now 'inform the basic structures of contemporary literature'.[10] Isherwood approaches this general and multivalent theme in a fresh way: his wish to enact religious searchings of identity through fiction gives a rare kind of novelist's insight into the existential.

Isherwood's standpoint is rare and individual for two main reasons. First, his homosexuality always affected his moral standpoint as a writer in that it caused a change of focus. The homosexual does not judge from the centre of the moral and social structure of his milieu. Second, Isherwood's religion is peculiarly flexible and eclectic, enabling him to be receptive to philosophies outside the European tradition of rationality and empiricism. As a result, the reification of much recent fiction is less present – only becoming part of the stylistic quality of *A Single Man*, which is largely concerned with the distance between self and others.

Other modes of being-in-the-world (Heidegger's phrase) of modern life do not concern him. The concept of 'The Absurd', for instance, is not directly relevant in the later fiction as the process and centrality of reason are not involved in this study. 'The Absurd is lucid reason noting its limits' (Camus: *The Myth of Sisyphus*) would not be applicable to George, Paul or Oliver, who are protagonists in a search for religious adherence to life and not simply the rational approach.

Isherwood also had to resolve the problem of the high seriousness in religious fiction. The introspective intensity and the discursive prose within much religious fiction was something he saw as a problem. He explains this in his essay on the religious novel:

> The mortification of the ego is tedious and painful. But I see no reason for the author to sentimentalise his hero's suffering, or to allow him to indulge in self-pity. Sports writers find no pathos in the hardships of a boxer's training.[11]

For these reasons I would answer yes to a question that has often been put about religious literature, most succinctly perhaps, by David Daiches:

> Has the contemporary literary artist anything to learn from this? (The classic writer's synthesis of literature and religion). Has the disintegration of community of belief which most observers agree to be a characteristic of our age altered the thing so radically that the kind of thing done by Aeschylus and Dante and Milton – posing questions suggested by religion and answering them in literary terms – become impossible?[12]

Certainly I would answer yes to the first question because Isherwood faces up to the issues raised in an age when faith has become a struggle to defeat not only the agnostic urge but also the idea of the self that wants to be bound by its involvement with reality only through maya.

Hinduism has three ways by which man may work towards the

freedom from self and the recognition of God within himself and in all life. It has jnana, which is knowledge; karma, which is action or service, and bhakti, which is devotion and prayer. It is a monistic religion which allows many approaches and views of the one Brahman or 'all-pervading god'. Also, the idea of 'Atman' is relevant to the themes in Isherwood's American novels. K. M. Sen explains it this way:

> Atman means self. *The Upanishads* point out that Brahman and Atman are the same. The Supreme has manifested himself in every soul, and the student of religion is dramatically told in that work: 'Tat tvam asi' (Thou art that).[13]

This view that denies the existence of the world as separate from God, is rooted in the *Upanishads*. The other main Hindu text, the *Bhagavad Gita*, however, stresses 'man's duties in the world' and it is the latter text that has most concerned Isherwood, in his religious fiction and in his autobiography. The idea of karma has more interest for him than that of bhakti. With his swami, he translated the *Gita*, the important Hindu epic, and he has written extensively on it. The branch of Hinduism called Vedanta is merely one philosophical system among many, taking the idea of Brahman as its central tenet, and Isherwood's religious fiction is primarily concerned with the recognition of Brahman through service to man and significant action in life. The devotion of bhakti as opposed to the service of karma is at the centre of *A Meeting by the River*. The most recent Vedantists have stressed that within the Brahman, the jiva, or individual soul, is to be properly understood. Sen explains this:

> Because of avidja (ignorance) the root of all troubles, the ego-feeling exists. The end is liberation and that is achieved through a practical realisation of the oneness of the self with the Absolute. If a person reaches this state he becomes jivan-mukta i.e. liberated while alive. Realising the oneness of all, his life becomes one of unselfish service.[14]

The notion of service or action is of central importance to Isherwood's work in the last four novels. Autobiographical experience is used to show the progression from Stephen Monk's Quaker 'service' to Oliver's more convincing understanding of duty to God in *A Meeting by the River*. In all these novels, the protagonists represent the failures of men to understand the link between the service of God and the love of humanity as part of the idea of Brahman.

In these four books, what is noticeable is the continual effort to impose a coherent design on the structure. In *The World in the Evening* he admits that he failed. When he was asked whether he intended anything specific in Monk's progress through the book he answered, 'Perhaps that's the whole trouble ... I don't like the character'.[15] This hints at a plan to use Monk as a representative for a clearly didactic purpose, even his name playing a part.

The design of a didactic fiction illustrating an abstract intellectual theme has been noted in *Down there on a Visit* also. Stuart Hampshire saw it as 'Isherwood's hell'[16] and in a letter to Edward Upward Isherwood writes. 'I receive dim adumbrations of quite a different sort of novel ... a journey which is not a journey ... something of the *Inferno*.[17] Isherwood's habit of trying to impose counterpoints of structure was still there (in the contrasts of Paul or Mr Lancaster with the narrator in the fashion of Dante and the inhabitants of hell, for instance) a pattern familiar from *The Memorial*. *A Meeting by the River* has its genesis in an abstract idea with symbolic suggestions: an idea of the Mexican border and two contrasting types of people in search of power on each side.

This approach does inhibit the newly developing study of self identity to some extent as the coherent design is usually a restrictive one, where the opposing characters become predictable. Monk is perhaps the best example of a figure who fails largely because his revolt from materialism is all too familiar in modern American fiction. The religious dimension is not interesting enough in its presentation and his homosexual relationship with Michael is too mean and jealous to win much respect for him when he leaves his second wife. He lacks the strength of intellect and integrity that Oliver has, for example.

However, the important thing that does occur in each of the religious novels is an attempt to explore the nature of transcendental experience, despite the fact that in his essay on the religious novel Isherwood states: 'Mystical experience itself can never be described. It can only be written around, hinted at, dimly reflected in word and deed'.[18] Consistent with this view, we see people in the greater part of these novels experiencing such feelings only by hints and inferences. The exception is with Oliver and Patrick in *A Meeting by the River*. As a result, the bulk of the novels is concerned also with that other consciousness that shows that the natural wakeful life of the ego is largely passivity. As Colin Wilson puts it: '. . . the main problem is the low pressure of everyday consciousness which rises only occasionally to moments of intense self-awareness'.[19] Isherwood has to stress this aspect of the subject of transcendence as he is not concerned with 'saints'.

These underlie the artistic and philosophic achievement of the major novels then: an examination of the knowledge of self of those who want freedom from the 'maya' and a search for a true understanding of the world that contains those fleeting things. As Juan Mascaro summarizes, the process of finding unselfishness leads to 'the realisation of the beautiful and the true'.[20]

Clearly, Isherwood knows the idealism behind such a statement, and he had to learn and ponder on such assertions from his swami. His own lack of resolution is a source of strength in the fiction. There is still, in this later writing, an ironic version of The Test that was mentioned earlier. The Hindu concept of karma involves a test of Isherwood's own conviction of The Truly Weak Man being the better artist. To indulge in hedonistic gratification and thus overrate the importance of maya at the expense of the spiritual, is not to be recommended in the 'evolution into higher consciousness'. A test of one's dominance over the will of the ego is the supreme test of these protagonists, and it was one that Isherwood had to cope with in life. His continuance of sexual love, for example, is reasoned into the observance of his faith as far as he followed his swami – for dogma could hardly be said to apply to his following of the way of Vedanta. A useful example of how much Isherwood wanted to tone down the intensity of the philosophical fiction that came from all this may be noted in his discussion of Larry in Maugham's *The Razor's Edge*.[21]

We must now trace the evolution of the above religious ideas through those novels which fail to achieve the right balance of ideology and realistic writing. To chart the course of failures is enlightening and adds to the assertion that the quality of his last two novels surpasses most of his earlier efforts quite considerably. *The World in the Evening* in the first section shows us Monk's subjection to a transient and hedonistic pleasure in serving a love that has failed. His second wife, Jane, has his allegiance only tenuously and we see him escape this false life that he hates into the retreat of the Quaker world of Sarah and his past. From the first page, Monk has reached the stage of questioning the moral responsibility of his self as a social, role-playing animal – a theme that recurs in all Isherwood's fiction:

> I was alone now, at the uncrowded end of the living-room. A mirror on the wall showed me how I appeared to the outside world . . . I look as if I was trying to melt into the scenery and become invisible . . . .[22]

This is his insecurity in a life that is no more than 'service' to a dead marriage. It is constantly contrasted with his inner attachment to his first wife (now dead), the writer, Elisabeth Rydal.

From this starting point, the scheme of the novel becomes too clumsily allegorical. It is a first attempt to express what is perfected in Patrick and Oliver: spiritual rebirth through what the character sees as true understanding of man and reality. Monk retreats to Sarah at the appropriately named 'Tawelfan' ('peaceful place' in Welsh) – and a place that becomes a soul's purgatory. Here the purgatorial preparation for rebirth into Atman is effected by means of the re-examination of the past motives of his wilful ego and his attachment to physical (homosexual) love.

Monk, in fact, is given many inner reflections which over-emphasize the symbolic representation of his past marriage as a trap and a grotesque prison:

> I got hot, then, thinking of them together; two mating giants filling the dwarf world of the doll's house, and nearly bursting it apart with their heavings and writhings.[23]

The wife and her lover, as he tormented them, are too clearly a symbol of a maya-life, the life of the senses that Monk is disgusted with. Tawelfan is his base for a close reassessment of his life with Elisabeth in which he discovers that, even with her, when he served the ideal of art, he was still in a prison: 'Yes, I admit it, you invented me. Until you told me who I was, I didn't begin to exist. I was the most lifelike of all your characters'.[24]

The Quaker life is examined also, and, despite his introverted scrutiny of his two roles as servant with the wives, Monk does not see the nature of the sect's work as anything but one more version of mindless duty and service. He makes Monk dissatisfied with the institutionalization of their church. He is distanced from Sarah: 'The Sarah-Stephen language had its limitations; there were many things you couldn't say in it at all'.[25]

Monk even has Gerda to draw his attention to the nature of the selfless life in a more personal sense, yet he is blind. Once again, Isherwood allows the symbolism of his imposed scheme to intrude. Elisabeth's best work was *The World in the Evening* and this conversation follows its mention when Monk and Gerda are talking of the past:

'The World in the evening? Die Welt am Abend .... Funny – that was also the name of a Communist newspaper in Berlin before Hitler came.' (Gerda)[26]

Thus suggesting that there are parallels between the world in general decline and in the personal life of Monk and Elisabeth. The past becomes a vehicle for expressing the length and depth of purgatory when one experiences the limits of ordinary consciousness. Monk is unable to accept circumstances and has the restlessness of the religious man: no more. He represents the type who cannot escape from 'avidya', ego-feeling. Monk's relationship with Michael is the core of this theme. He has the will to escape and come to true understanding, but like Dante's Belaqua, he is unable to assert his will. Monk often expresses his dissatisfaction with this ego-feeling: 'That house was always swarming with people and cocktails and hangovers; and the laziness and the drifting drove me nearly frantic with guilt'.[27]

As the reader is led to expect, Monk cannot even understand Sarah without tuition from Gerda. The question of her faith is his final defeat:

What Sarah believes in, I believe in that. (Gerda)
But you just said that you didn't .... (Monk)
I know. It does not make any sense. I only know this: what Sarah believes, this is true. (Gerda)

You mean, true for her? (Monk)
No, true for all. Because it is SHE who believes. (Gerda)[28]

Monk is unable to understand. Gerda takes the role of teacher.
Monk sees Gerda's perception briefly (p. 323) and he is coming
out of his ignorance. The book is the purgatory in Isherwood's
scheme of the study of the self through fiction: what constitutes,
for Monk, the experience of purgatory, is the capture of the
present by the past.

It is not really important that Sarah be convincing (as Angus
Wilson insists she should)[29] as the other characters need not
learn from her in any detailed way. Nevertheless, the novel is
the most forthright and least subtle of the four religious novels.
The theme of the self dedicated to the service of man is seen in
many forms which develop concurrently and Monk's feeble
character is not enough to make Gerda and the rest convincing
in their roles as his teachers. However, it is a first attempt. Monk
is, because of his effort to escape from the maya of the sensual
world by the end of the novel, the first of the protagonists who
show the characteristics of the first of the four men mentioned in
Gita:

> There are four kinds of men who are good and the four love
> me, Arjuna: the man of sorrows, the seeker after knowledge,
> the seeker of something he treasures and the man of vision.[30]

These themes are further explored in *Down there on a Visit* and
in a most interesting way, for Isherwood goes back into his past
once more and it is by the narrator's meeting with various
suffering people or 'self-imprisoned' people that we learn that
'Down there' is – a series of scenes that do have a similarity in
theme to Dante's visit to hell with Virgil. The book has been
judged as four accounts of loneliness within mental states of hell
(as in Sartre's *In Camera*). Brian Finney commented that, 'It is
equally about Christopher's penetration beneath the various
strata of the ego to the awareness of being conscious . . .'.[31]

The strata of the ego here are to be observed in the search for
knowledge of the world, in various ways, as each man assumes
that knowledge is in some way an answer to the doubts of the
security of existence. Lancaster is supposedly learned and clever
but only on the surface; Ambrose wants knowledge of people in

a form of sacrifice to him; Paul asks for the ultimate knowledge of the transcendental through the punishment of the body. Each shows the self in an absolute desire for possession: of self-pride, of the transient wealth of the world and of other people respectively.

The book begins with the statement of the relativity of the self; the narrator being distanced. We need this distancing if we are to judge the failures in relation to a guide who submits and suffers with them. We are about to be shown the attachment to illusory maya which is keeping these men, like Stephen Monk, in their purgatory. Once more, like the Beckettian protagonist, the men here are attached to trivial possessions and obsessions and these become a substitute for the effort towards self-understanding (cf. Beckett's heroine in *Happy Days* for a dramatic portrayal of a similar idea).

They are like detailed accounts of Beckett's Malone with his escape from self-knowledge:

> I have rummaged a little in my things, sorting them out and drawing them over to me, to look at them. I was not far wrong in thinking that I knew them off by heart, and could speak of them at any moment without looking at them.[32]

Malone is only Ambrose or Paul without society. When Ambrose says to 'Isherwood': 'After all, lovey, I'm dead and you aren't', we know that this man, with his creation of life on his island, is really only decorating his 'chamber in hell'.

Mr Lancaster, too, is imprisoned in his self-delusion and attachment to the sensual world. In his suspended state he is in the Beckettian state of self, without grace: 'He had lived too long within his own sounding-box, listening to his own reverberations. He didn't need me'.[33]

Isherwood clearly wanted to say farewell to his narrator-persona of the earlier books, and it is an effective way to do so when he is made a guide through the hell of 'Down there'. The most informative statement by the narrator in this respect is that he is genuinely a rebel. He knows instinctively that it is 'only by rebellion that he will ever learn and grow'.[34] He is rebelling from his former social self, his group of familiar roles, as his tour across Europe shows. He began the book, of course, visiting Lancaster in the capacity of 'nephew' and assumed a role on the

ship that was not sincere. The narrator becomes a man in his
own hell also, in the Waldemar section. It is, again, a kind of
isolation but this time very social, unlike the others. He is at his
furthest from God, or grace, in one of these places of 'unbeing'
where the idea of self-knowledge is unknown: 'When I hear the
word "God" it makes me want to vomit . . . it describes everything that's filthy . . .'.[35]

The first three sections extend Isherwood's earlier subject-
matter of the ties of hedonism and maya and the inability to
escape from moral responsibility to others and the service of
man. It is in the long section, *Paul*, that we really find the man of
the *Gita* who is the seeker after self-knowledge:

> In his essay on 'Hypothesis and Belief', Isherwood says, 'Life
> contains a number of vivid sense-pleasures, and the gaps of
> despondency and boredom between them can be filled more
> or less adequately by hard work, sleep, the movies, drink and
> day-dreaming.'[36]

It is the waiting in limbo that is the existential problem for the
man who refuses the search for self-knowledge: like Vladimir
and Estragon in Beckett's *Waiting for Godot*, the spiritual land-
scape is bare. For Isherwood, the convinced materialist will
'commit suicide'. Here we have Paul. The story is a detailed
account of our guide's relationship with a man who is able to
impel his will from the waiting to an attempt at going beyond the
Gita's 'mysterious cloud of appearances' that form maya for
invalid reasons (an idea also developed in Isherwood's short
story, *A Visit to Anselm Oakes*).

It is in *Paul* that Isherwood first really develops the study of
the duality of perception of our being-in-the-world that matures
in *A Meeting by the River*. The relevant concept in Vedanta is
explained by G. A. Feuerstein:

> According to the ontological conception of the *Gita* the sub-
> ject and the object of the spatio-temporal world are both
> rooted and intersect in the ultimate reality. They are the two
> poles of the One Being experiencing itself.[37]

This element of the Vedanta idea of self is the central one in the
later novels. Isherwood's fiction gradually expresses these ideas

more intensely and in terms of polarities as he shows us the opposite selves meeting.

At the opening of *Paul*, and periodically through the story, we are aware of self and other (purusa and praktri) experiencing 'itself':

> When I first set eyes on Paul ... I remember I noticed his strangely erect walk; he seemed almost paralytic with tension ... I'm waiting to see if he'll do anything to interest me; and I almost believe he knows this. I feel, at any rate, that he's capable of knowing it.[38]

What develops is a test – that familiar feature of the Isherwood-narrator's self's submission to the acknowledgement of 'other' in itself. In not yielding to Paul's test of him in the hotel room sex invitation – by maintaining his 'self-respect' – the narrator has invited Paul to meet him on his own terms; and so their coming-together in their sexual relationship begins. This also acts as – eventually – an excuse to introduce a study of that eccentric and influential teacher, Gerald Heard, into the fiction under the name of Augustus Parr. However, despite these biographical factors, the true theme of the story develops into Paul as the man seeking after knowledge. In *Bhagavad Gita 7*, Krishna places the man of vision above all others but Isherwood is not concerned with him here: he keeps to the men who have restless life – one of Krishna's three 'guras': the three states of the soul:

> And know that the three guras, the three states of the soul, come from me: peaceful light, restless life and lifeless dark-ness. But I am not in them: they are in me.[39]

There is a remarkable closeness here to these men in 'hell' within themselves. Paul is not in 'lifeless darkness' – that suits Mr Lancaster more. Paul is able to try to join the narrator in his efforts and visits Parr, the teacher. But Paul is also, because of this 'restless life' as the narrator's 'praktri' (other), used as a first step in exploring the themes of identity in the religious novel.

As it deals with the search for Atman and higher conscious-ness, the story also allows Paul to play the part of 'devil's advocate' to the ideas of conversion and faith:

'Parr has a beard, doesn't he?' Paul asked this in his demurest, least ironical manner . . . . But I wasn't going to let myself be provoked. 'Yes, he has a beard, yes, and he's a bit Christlike . . . . He's vainly human and he's no fool, and at the same time he really believes . . . .'
'Just what does he believe?'[40]

The attempt to undermine the assertion of belief and the story's remarkable parallels with Vedanta ideas come to a head later in this scene. Paul asks:

'Why should any ordinary, sensible person want to get in touch with this thing – as you call it?'
'Because it's – that's what life's for.'
'Who says so?'
'Well, I mean – what else can it be for – except to find out who you really are?'
'What makes you think it's for anything? Why can't it just be a filthy mess of meaningless shit?'[41]

In this way the 'tests' are effected, testing pride and vanity, until Paul thinks he is persuaded into faith of a kind. His many adventures into immorality have been his restless life in search of self-knowledge. He then unites with the other, the narrator, when they live and pray together.

Then the test of service with the Quakers arrives and Paul cannot accept or submit to service as duty to man. The dissolution of the relationship is the falling away of the lower self (apara praktri) from the higher. The allegory behind this is similar to that of *The World in the Evening* (see above). The whole point of the allegory of the soul lost in dissolution is stated at the close of the story where the narrator goes 'down there' to Hell again where the 'other' is dying. Just before Paul's physical death, the narrator sees him:

The Paul who appeared that evening had a sinister, sepulchral elegance; Dorian Gray arisen from the tomb. Paul ate only caviar . . . but also drank only several cocktails. I reminded him that he had spoken against alcohol that afternoon. 'I know darling,' he answered, with a touch of impatience, 'but I find I just cannot talk unless I drink . . . alcohol brings my mind down to the level of other people.'[42]

The summing up comes with the short statement by Ronny: 'he had a genius for enjoying himself' (ibid).

There is, then, an account here of what must be sacrificed for the attempt at real self-knowledge to be gained. The harmony of the two polarities of self cannot be demonstrated in this social context as Isherwood still felt autobiography to be intrusive, as in the use he made of Parr/Heard as the teacher. This point is vital to the understanding of Isherwood's later work: he learned, after this work, to separate the fiction of his religious novels from his obsession with the self as studied in straight-forward autobiography. From now on his work divides more clearly into these two modes.

The result of these first two religious novels is that they show the failures – the men who are in Krishna's terms 'of the self' but not able to know transcendence, or even properly attempt it. In the end, I believe, the affirmation of the joy in Vedanta teachings was the reason for such intense and prolonged self-study. These two novels detail the self-tortured man who knows unattainable states of being but cannot achieve them, of whom Aldous Huxley says:

> He identifies himself with his pain, and in becoming merely the awareness of his suffering body, is delivered from that sense of past guilt and present frustration, that anxiety about the future which constitutes so large a part of the neurotic ego.[43]

Huxley here recognizes what Isherwood perceives as the central idea of 'the sense of past guilt' being an influential part of self-identity and the search for Atman. It is interesting to note that Karma may be translated as 'action' or as 'guilt'. This suggests that all the actions of the people in these novels represent the two concepts simultaneously: that wrong, immoral action is the source of guilt as it is not 'the proper way' unless it is service of man with the recognition that service is part of one's own will to share divinity (the central idea of *A Meeting by the River* also). This is the very point at which the *Gita* begins: with the moral dilemma posed by a battlefield where the Lord warrior Arjuna suddenly perceives the pointlessness of his actions as killers of men.

A summary of the first religious novels must therefore emphasize the relation between Isherwood's evident intention to show a religious and ontological dimension to the modern amoral social man and the general and multifarious literary preoccupations with the alienation of man and his divorce from the reasoned meaning of objective reality found in Existential writings especially.

Isherwood, after his assumption of a life directed largely, but not totally, by Vedanta, wrote a kind of fiction in which alternative modes to those of Existentialism's exploration of the self are to be found. This is not to suggest, however, that he wrote in a consciously didactic way. I have merely noted some parallels between the fiction and the religious teachings. These first two novels dealing with religious themes are clearly an attempt to clarify Isherwood's own mind on the issues also.

The Hindu concepts of Atman, polarities of self, karma and maya all help in understanding the real depth of the communication in these novels. After all, the underlying attempt is one that aims to convey a spiritual odyssey of a Western mind into an alien Eastern faith. Isherwood tries to depict men without self-knowledge and without the ability or desire to begin such a search as Oliver's. What they all share, however, is the quality of 'rajas' – where all is dominated by self-assertiveness, the will of the ego.

6
The Religious Novel and the Transcendental Self

In *A Meeting by the River* and *A Single Man* Isherwood attempts religious and existential themes, once more related to his pre-occupation with self-identity, but now, because of his religious study, (conversion is not perhaps the right word), the themes attempt to show the transcendental experience and the physical isolation of man; the polarization of the spiritual and the sensual.

As a starting point, the general existential trends of a great deal of fiction in the fifties and sixties must be briefly considered in relation to the nature of transcendental experience. The most comprehensive survey of this is in Colin Wilson's *The Outsider* where the chapter on 'Breaking the Circuit' presents the case for the transcendental as a counterbalance to the numerous writers of existential tradition from Barbusse to Sartre which has been a social and purely secular attempt to understand the nature of self and being in relation to an absurd and Godless creation. Wilson uses the terms 'religious man' and 'imaginative man' to characterize his outsider – but one who is outside 'any specific religious system'. The figure fails in the struggle to understand being and meaning because he insists on seeing the world in pessimistic terms according to Wilson. The only writers that Wilson can introduce into his argument in order to study the transcendental are the mystics: T. E. Hulme, Traherne and Gurdieff, but he includes some discussion of Ramakrishna and his experience of transcendence: a sudden vision of the unity of all life under the Absolute (pp. 275–82). This is no different from the Western idea – or indeed, experience, of such a state – but the vision is expressed with great clarity and simplicity. It is significant, however, that no religious novel which deals with the transcendental is examined. Hesse's *Steppenwolf* is cursorily mentioned, but gradually an argument develops that dismisses the novel as an art form that has dealt adequately with mystical experience.

It needed thinkers like Martin Buber and the Theistic Existentialists to accommodate the transcendental, paradoxically in writing that has been creatively analytic, as if imaginative treatment is the only suitable medium for such speculation. As Richard Sheppard says:

> The Angst which haunts the Existentialist world derives from a conflict between the suppressed dimension of conscious which seeks to express itself in terms appropriate to itself . . . . Self expression saves them from Nihilism. Surrendering to the 'fallen world' existence precedes essence – a possibility of living authentically according to self-created values. Buber sees authentically in attunement to an existence according to the timeless moments which are generated when the Eternal Thou breaks into time through the Human Thou.[1]

Here Sheppard succinctly puts the case for the transcendental experience as an important addition to the numerous perceptions and 'self-created values' of the protagonists of modern Existential fiction.

When Isherwood first considered the religious novel that had to deal with saints and mystical experience, in his essay, *The Problem of the Religious Novel*, his touchstones were Dostojevsky's Father Zossima in *The Brothers Karamazov* and Somerset Maugham's Larry in *The Razor's Edge*. His concern in this essay is to discuss the difficulty of converting a fictional character convincingly into a 'saint' (his word) or mystic. The idea of the quest for truth and self-knowledge in a novel such as *Siddhartha* did not appeal to him, or he had no knowledge of Hesse, and what is interesting is that *The Razor's Edge*, about which he has a lot to say, is dependent on the social realism and contrasting character portrayals – just the things that Isherwood had shown he needed in the 'failures' (his own summing up) of *The World in the Evening*.

In *A Meeting by the River* it is clear that Isherwood wanted to explore the polarities of the spiritual and the physical, dealing with the nature of the transcendental at the very centre of

the themes. This motivation is supported by his remarks to
R. Wennersten:

> *A Meeting by the River* grew out of an idea that I'd had for a
> long time, which was a dialogue between two people with very
> different symbolic backgrounds. If you like: Jesus and Satan
> in the wilderness or any other two power-figures who confront
> each other.[2]

What developed from this germ of the theme was the necessity
of trying to describe and 'annotate' the process of the transcendental experience in order to show the source of the 'power' in
one of the two, Oliver: the modern reader would be all too well
acquainted with the source of Patrick's (the wordly man's)
power.

It is clear from the essay on the religious novel that the preoccupation with identity which may be observed in all Isherwood's fiction in some form, now begins to mature fully, for he
has to tackle the nature of a perception which is a recognizably
religious one: one that changes minds and lives and had indeed
changed his own, albeit gradually. In *Prater Violet* the 'Christopher' had ended his narrative with something close to the Existentialist 'adventure' of Sartre's Roquentin in *La Nausée*, where
some authenticity is found through creativity. This is a negative
consolation by the standards of those who believe in the value of
transcendence, and Isherwood, in order to express his profound
curiosity about, and belief in, the Hindu concept of the Absolute ('Brahman'), had to define what kind of *Bildungsroman*
could contain the characters of Oliver and Patrick in his 'power
struggle'. As I indicate above, he had few criteria for judgement
in his mind when it cam to understanding the religious novel. In
my view, he chose the variety of transcendental experience
which is most universally documented: that of Ramakrishna,
Traherne and so on, but he was also aware, as a practitioner of
meditation, that in a lesser form, such experience was part of
routine: the sustenance of faith, keeping the idea of the loss of
the lower self (in Hindu terms) momentarily, in meditation.

There have been many interpretations of the transcendental
experience and many different terminologies have been used. It
is necessary here to define those which Isherwood understood
and employed, in order to perceive how the themes of self-

knowledge come to their logical conclusion in a positive form in this novel. I suggest that the following types of transcendental experience have been described: the religious-mystical; the Theistic Existential and the expanded consciousness of perception (termed 'privileged moments' by E. F. N. Jephcott: see below).

The first is clearly described by C. S. Lewis, who uses the simple word 'joy' for this perception:

> We mortals, seen as the sciences see us and as we commonly see each other, are mere 'appearances'. But appearances of the Absolute. In so far as we really are at all we have, so to speak, a root in the Absolute, which is the utter reality. And that is why we experience joy: we yearn rightly for that unity which we can never reach except by ceasing to be the separate phenomenal beings called 'we'.[3]

This is perhaps the most common explanation: that universal unity is the main perception. It is similar to that of Rama-krishna, whose life and work Isherwood was familiar with. He saw a flight of cranes fly over a paddy field and 'It presented such a beautiful contrast that my mind wandered to far-off regions. Lost to outward sense, I fell down . . .'.[4] His mental conscious-ness had left him and become 'one with Brahman'.

Theistic Existentialism, as in the work of Buber and Jaspers, sees the participation of isolated self and greater unity as being more active: 'Timeless moments' are somehow 'generated' when Buber's Eternal meets the human. Jaspers perceives the importance of this as a force that overcomes the fragmentation that constantly assails personality.

Finally, there is the interest of the artist in transcendence, or the use of it, in art. Here, the study of such experience in the lives of Rilke and Proust by E. F. N. Jephcott is helpful. Jeph-cott terms these insights 'privileged moments' and bases his study on the descriptions of Baudelaire and Valéry, encom-passing also Sartre in *La Nausée*. His remarks on Roquentin are relevant here:

> Roquentin's existence is even more arid and monotonous than that of Lord Chandos (in Hofmannstal) but it is illuminated at rare intervals by moments of inexplicable abundance . . . 'I seem to have reached the summit of my happiness . . .'.[5]

Jephcott adds that privileged moments occur 'as a kind of arbitrary grace; and they involve a state of being which . . . is immeasurably superior in everyday life' (ibid.). The fundamental difference between this intellectual epiphany and that of (say) Ramakrishna, or Oliver in *A Meeting by the River*, is that the latter take the perception as a force which extends and fulfils – and is accepted as another dimension to consciousness as natural and valid as the nature of the routine 'robot consciousness' as Wilson calls the actions of role play and automatic actions.

For Jephcott there is the further awareness of the notion of abstract concepts and the sense of identity disappearing in these states:

> In a privileged moment these concepts disappear: 'Everything ceases to have its ordinary effect and what we guide ourselves by tends to vanish. There are . . . no names to such things'.[6]

Isherwood understood this (and the related drug experiences through his contact with Huxley) and he has given us his version in the opening of *A Single Man* where George has an intense perception of his physical nature: he is no longer anything more than a set of biological functions. As will be seen in the next section, George is the man who is embedded in existential quandary, unable to 'become': the Beckettian 'attendant'.

Having examined these concepts briefly, it is important now to isolate the nature of Oliver: he experiences the more orthodox religious epiphany but Isherwood has to explore the non-religious version – the privileged moment – too, in Patrick's experience. For Isherwood, as for Jung, the transcendental has this quality: 'Absolute certainty brings its own evidence and has no need of anthropomorphic proofs'. His fictional problem was not easily resolved as, for this reason of such proofs not being lucidly explained, adequate language was not available to describe such things.

Isherwood insisted on thinking in terms of 'saints' and Oliver is conscious of his having such a tag, which is successfully exploited fictionally as he is that paradox, the vain and seemingly affected person who finally and genuinely succeeds in his quest for faith and self-knowledge. The saint, says Isherwood, has motives of fear, vanity and desire and is unpredictable. This helps in defining what transcendence had to be.

Isherwood had not only his basic sense of the context of his fiction being founded on social reality, but he had also an example in print at the time he was reflecting on how to write about such an elusive topic. This was Maugham's *The Razor's Edge* (1944). He refers to this often and was in fact consulted by Maugham when he was planning the novel. There are remarkable similarities in the two novels: Maugham sets up several contrasts in terms of self-identity. Larry is one person in a group of wealthy hedonists who wishes to understand existence more profoundly. In contrast, the narrator, Elliot, and Sophie are used in order to reduce the 'saintly' Larry to humanity every time he appears to take a significant step towards Atman. The novel deals with the nature of Hinduism and its impact on the Western mind and it also explores the transcendental as a means of 'conversion'. Like Oliver, Larry knows the compulsions of sensuality and also feels the suffering in the world very deeply.

More important are the stylistic devices of the two novels. Both rely greatly on the use of a mock-autobiographical scheme or background. Where Isherwood uses the intimacy of the epistolatory novel. Maugham inserts himself as narrator and controls the reader's opinions by selective information about Larry at important moments. At the end, Larry and the narrator undergo a confrontation with values which has all the absolute polarities of the moral behaviour of Oliver and Patrick. Also, neither can avoid being burdened by the need to explain, in dialogue, the nature of Hinduism. The transcendental perceptions of the two protagonists actually occur only briefly, and both in a context of explanation to themselves of the experience:

> I knew that Swami was 'dead', and I knew that nevertheless he was now with me – and that he is with me always, wherever I am . . . I woke up actually knowing that. I can't say that I still know it, in that absolute sense, as I write these words, but at least I can still vividly remember how I felt at the time. My eyes keep filling with tears of joy remembering it.[7]

and:

> . . . The sun caught the lake through a cleft in the heights and it shone like burnished steel. I was ravished with the beauty of the world. I'd never known such exaltation and such a transcendent joy . . . when I came to myself I was trembling.[8]

Both novels are concerned with doubt and scepticism as much as with belief. The narrative styles make this possible. Maugham ends by discounting Larry's difference from, or superiority over, the worldly people by saying, 'For all the persons with whom I have been concerned got what they wanted ... and we, the public, all like a success story'.[9]

Isherwood allows the possibility of the equality of Oliver's and Patrick's epiphanies, and this is important. A writer may explain what it is like to experience transcendental joy without making us feel it. This problem, I suggest, is central to the problem that he faced in this novel and other such fiction. It is a linguistic problem – regarding the inadequacy of language – and Isherwood only found part of the answer in explaining what this experience is not: the negative statements of *A Single Man*. (See the next section.) Even though *A Meeting by the River* apparently explains the transcendental, in fact, it does more: it also presents a case for such an epiphany being ordinary as well as purely religious, and Oliver's training and discipline are no better preparation for this than Patrick's life-experience and emotional responses.

It is useful here to compare the above accounts of such experience with the method used by Hesse in *Siddhartha*. Hesse uses a series of images and explanations of feelings, in the third person, throughout. The images are conventional and within Hindu tradition, like the powerful symbol of the river and the ferryman for instance. When Hesse comes to try and explain the transcendental insights, he does not isolate the feelings in order to heighten them sharply as Isherwood or Maugham do: he merely describes in greater analytic detail:

> Siddhartha listened. He was now listening intently, completely absorbed, quite empty, taking in everything. He felt that he had now completely learned the art of listening. He had often heard all this before, all these numerous voices in the river, but today they sounded different. He could no longer distinguish the different voices .... They were all interwoven and interlocked. All the voices, all the goals, all the yearnings, all the sorrows, all the pleasure, all the good and evil, all of them together was the world ... then the great song of a thousand voices consisted of one word: om – perfection.[10]

Despite the detail of impression and feeling, the effect is still objective. There is still no personalizing of the whole experience that transmits the emotional content to the reader. Isherwood and Maugham do similar things but the really significant factor in Isherwood is that it is not Oliver's but Patrick's epiphany that has more subjective feeling, as it is more easily identifiable with the reader's knowledge – lacking the vocabulary of religious ceremony. The material of love poetry or of Wordsworth's 'Intimations of Immortality' are closer to this than any theology. An example of this is in the slow build-up to Patrick's change of ideals and his understanding of love, when he writes to Tom:

> Oh Tommy what can I say to you? There's too much to say. And I'm thinking about you so hard, all words seem meaningless. That afternoon down on the reef at Tunnel Cove, with the air full of spray and the shock of the waves making the rock tremble – no, if I talk about that I shall break the magic. It WAS magic, wasn't it, every time we were together .... When I'm with you I'm quite a different person.[11]

As the reader has before him a man who breaks away from emotional attachments, his change and insights into himself and the nature of love mean more, subjectively, than the very analytical perceptions of Oliver, despite Oliver's insistence on the quality of emotion in his experience after his swami dies. This problem is a difficult one to resolve, of course, and there have been many fictional attempts to emotionalize and explain the transcendental experience, especially in children's fiction, but Jung's statement (above, p. 83) always hinders satisfactory explanation.

The importance of *The Razor's Edge* is that it taught Isherwood the way to deal with writing about transcendence in universal terms: the characterization which moves away from either stereotypes or eccentrics took a long time to achieve. His criticism of Maugham shows what he learned: 'One gets the impression that becoming a saint is just no trouble at all'.

Despite all Maugham's efforts to show the essence of a person changing and becoming a 'saint' and his use of the contrast of polarities, Isherwood clearly saw that *The Razor's Edge* did not delve deeply enough into what Isherwood's Vedanta saw as Purusa and Praktri: 'Self and Other' which are the two poles of the one being. His idea of the absolutes of sensual, physical being on the one hand and of spiritual being on the other needed to be more clearly structured in Patrick and Oliver rather than using Maugham's occasional hints that Larry had 'Jesus and the devil in him' – in the sense that Larry's 'goodness' had the power to ruin others.

For these reasons, I hope to show that in *A Meeting by the River* Isherwood has created an account of the nature of self-identity which is a logical outcome of the earlier novels and in fact continues past preoccupations in a more profound way. He wrote of all the common methods of escape from self-knowledge which appear at first to be variations on the general Existential fictional patterns of recent fiction – such as Stephen Monk's new life after leaving his second wife and finding an 'authenticity' which is a common theme in, for instance, Wain and Amis and in much recent American fiction. However, in order to perfect the attempt of *The World in the Evening* in presenting any account of a new life being reached through an epiphany, he needed the simplicity of form that an epistolary novella gives. He produced a work that confronts the problem of how to *a*) show that the transcendental is a universal human mode of self-knowledge, and *b*) use the realism of his customary methods to fulfil the needs of a religious novel as he saw these in his essay on that topic.

We must now examine the novel and its points of contact with *A Single Man* in order to demonstrate his measure of success in these aims. My previous sections have noted Isherwood attempting to make of his egocentric fiction a series of allegorical patterns and realistic/documentary fictional schemes. This egocentricity changed and extended its scope as Isherwood's faith in Vedanta and its practical value to life developed. The attempt to deal with religious experience in *The World in the Evening* was marred by over-emphasis on the idea of action – so vital to the idea of Vedanta and of Quakerism (in which he had been briefly involved as a volunteer worker). *A Meeting by the River* is an extension of these concerns into a more concentrated exploration of transcendence as yet another aspect of the study of self-identity.

The novel may be approached by listing three apparent intentions which all relate to the central theme of transcendence: the desire for the selflessness of action, in terms of duty and service;

the essential paradox and humour in the human aspiring to the 'saintly'; and the nature of the two polarities of selfishness and the relinquishment of possession and will.

The plot is ideal for these intentions to be explored to the full. Two 'power-figures' are seen at work deeply embedded in the most universally observed human situation: the family and its morality – which maintains the interest begun in his first novel. Here, Isherwood's homosexuality helps to bring the themes out in an unusual way, as Patrick has to revolt from his early, seeming security and contentment and his homosexual relationship enables him to have the exit route when his epiphany comes. In addition, the vanity and fear that Isherwood sees as essential to the saint are easily pinpointed in a familial intricacy of pretence and deception, allowing Patrick and Oliver to deceive others and themselves. They must have vanities and fears in order to lose them and to show a radical change later.

For the first half of the novel we read of a man who is vain and defensive yet eager to fulfil some drive towards a life of 'service'. He has taken a decisive step which he hopes will change his life and self. We then receive a cruel and seemingly biased account of this man and we find him unconvincing – a mere dilettante in religion. This enables Isherwood to concentrate on making Oliver pompous, as the necessity of his teaching Patrick (and his readers) about the niceties of life as a swami produces an unsureness and artificiality in him.

Nevertheless, there is an intense desire for goodness and service in Oliver. His certainty as to this is given early in the book: 'You only had to choose between social service and private selfishness'.[12] Of course, the long diary entries that Oliver makes begin to develop the irony which is maintained to the end. We see their mutual understanding and thus the humour, which Isherwood noted as essential in his essay on the religious novel.

From the beginning, Oliver is casting off his former self – the person who was Oliver and American and so on – to assume his new self of swami. In the diaries we perceive his growing into belief through reflection. Service for others, extremely active and dedicated, has been his need but he had suddenly understood that service to his God is the real and significant thing.

Furthermore, the diary and letter method of plot enables Isherwood to maintain the humour which is so essential if 'Mr

Jones is to become a saint and be believable' as he says in his essay on the religious novel. Their humour is, though, rather forced most of the time which very subtly betrays the unease of both men:

> I am not and never shall be incommunicado, as you suggest. This monastery is not run by Trappists! You ask if I shall ever come to England again. That's a question I can't definitely answer at present . . . .[13]

This offhand, only partly natural tone keeps the future swami firmly fixed as a possibility in the present Oliver; even his humour is strained when asked to admit that he is still the familiar figure whom Patrick knows. Irony gradually gains depth and power as these techniques increase in many guises. The overall result is that Oliver is self-conscious of his change in life-style and identity as Patrick gradually adapts his roles to counter his brother. These stylistic devices are ideal for the meeting by the 'river' which is also a hint of frontier as well as the Hindu image of time and creation: a frontier here where Christ and Satan meet (see above notes on the genesis of the novel).

The success of the central themes of the novel depends on the clear separateness of Oliver and Patrick while both are nevertheless transformed by radical and revelatory experience. What Isherwood does in order to reveal gradually the nature of each revelation of the transcendental is to use two paradoxes: in Patrick's case his experience emerges from a life-style in which his homosexual love for Tom has seemed shallow and even unconvincing to him as he investigates it deeper – and he is made comical in his views of and responses to boys (see p. 68) yet his love for Tom is the very source of the revelation:

> This was much more than a dream, it was so intense it was a sort of vision. I mean, there was a burning pleasure and then an utter fulfilment with you . . . . But the whole experience went far beyond just sex, it was actually a glimpse of a life which you and I were living together . . . this life I got a glimpse of was of such a closeness as I'd never even imagined could exist between two human beings because it was a life entirely without fear.[14]

The long-term consequences of this vision are his liberation from that very fear that he sees in most relationships (by inference from this statement): his family duties and moral obligations that have characterized his thoughts and actions through a great deal of his letters and reflections on earlier life. The corresponding paradox is with Oliver, who is again unsure of his transcendental experience of the swami and his 'daemon' until later, at the end of the book, when he is shown the certainty that his rebirth into the priesthood is the right path for him. To extend the paradox even further, both brothers appear to understand each other's condition perfectly. Oliver knows that Patrick is in 'a state of grace and he's going to discover it the hard way' (p. 142). Patrick tells Oliver outright that he lives 'a life totally without fear' (p. 126) and the claim is made by Oliver that the swami daemon is working for both men's new lives.

All this concern for a humorous and demystified basis, in which he must keep his 'saint' believable, demands that Patrick has a particular duality in himself from which to emerge, so that the contrast with Oliver is more profound. This is Patrick's homosexuality – or, rather, bisexuality. He is two men with two emotional attachments. Isherwood has long been involved with the place of the homosexual in society, of course, but here Patrick takes on the role of apologist for a deviation – one just as marginal, suspect and eccentric (in the literal sense) as the minority of American converts to Hinduism.

Patrick's letters to Tommy and his wife reveal a man who has the traits of the minority member summarized by Mailer (see above, section 4). His self-understanding emerges from his virtual idolatry of Tommy. He is, in fact, intolerably patronizing when he breaks free of homosexual involvement and in this important passage he also comes to a knowledge of his errors:

> Being married does make a lot of things easier, because the world accepts marriage at its face value, without asking what goes on behind the scenes – whereas it's always a bit suspicious of bachelors! The unmarried are apt to regard marriage as a prison – actually it gives you greater freedom.[15]

Isherwood makes us see this discussion as part of Patrick's gradual rebirth through his experience, and Patrick himself sees it as renunciation of something: 'It's true what they call renunciation is what we would call rejection of responsibility, but nevertheless, it isn't an easy thing to do.' (p. 106).

We have in this novel, then, an examination of how two polarities of the concept of self-identity, the spiritual and physical, may each find its own kind of transcendental understanding and a kind of rebirth: one in a 'teacher' role and one in a 'student' role. However, by the structure of the novel and the several juxtapositions of ironical humour, two things are finally resolved. First, the problem of the portrayal of transcendental experience in a realistic context as opposed to the lyricism of *Siddhartha* or even the types of this shown through the genre of fantasy by Stephen Donaldson in *Lord Foul's Bane*. Second, the concepts of duty and service for mankind, as in the teachings of Vedanta, have been studied fictionally – much more successfully than in *The World in the Evening*.

Oliver's original assumption that 'you only had to choose between social service and private selfishness' is demolished and the problem resolved when his life in the priesthood begins and he has understood karma, the concept of true action and service. Again in terms of Vedanta, Oliver and Patrick have gained not only self-knowledge but the important further stage of this, jivan-mukta:

> Because of avidya (ignorance), the root of all troubles, the ego-feeling exists. The end is liberation and that is achieved through a practical realisation of the oneness of the self with the Absolute. If a person reaches this state he becomes jivan-mukta – liberated while alive ... his life becomes one of unselfish service.[16]

Isherwood, then, not only gives us an imaginative account of how an ordinary person emerges from doubt and egoistic assumptions – 'The very idea of mysticism set my teeth on edge' (p. 17) – to a knowledge of life through the transcendental, but also gives us a portrait of how the man who is not even 'called' to religion is saved similarly (as in Saint Paul). The profound effect that Vedanta had on Isherwood's life also penetrated his art to the extent that he clearly had to trace the course of the loss of 'private selfishness'. The concepts of Vedanta helped greatly in this aim being accomplished, but of course one has to bear in mind reservations about the problem of language and feeling involved, as I discuss above. There is no doubt, also, that the novel solves the problem of the religious novel as he posed the questions about the genre in his speculative essay, 'The Problem of the Religious Novel', mentioned above.

It would be easy, of course, to raise doubts as to the supposed validity of the experiences that change these protagonists' minds, but all I assert here is that the evidence in the novel suggests that it is, overall, a more successful study of the subject than the previous novel. It is, for my purposes, proof that there was yet another dimension in the fictional study of identity that had possible answers, although it does not provide absolute conclusions. The religious novel that does this would be, I suggest, almost impossible to find.

7

'A Single Man': The Prison of Selfhood

I have reached the stage where Isherwood's fictional oeuvre has progressed from social realism and the study of identity in a familial setting to an extremely personal perception of the possibility of transcendence. As his writing life continued, he always used fiction as an alternative to autobiography for the judgement of experience, and always at the centre of his fiction is the Isherwood surrogate who has grown imaginatively from the original thoughts and events of diary notes. His interviews always suggest the closeness of diary and fiction; and of course his recent autobiographical works have had diaries as source material. In his last two novels we have his most profound statements about the polarities of self which have been important in this study: the physical and spiritual in man. In the previous section, transcendental experience was contrasted with the materialist and sensual human motivations, but no real study of the self identity that is perceived outside social ties and is demarcated by physical being had been attempted in earlier fiction. In *A Single Man* he attempts this.

In many ways, the novel is exploratory of common themes in American literature as a whole: the nature of a minority; the liberation of the individual; and the lack of communication between age-groups, but these are all of secondary importance. The novel is primarily Isherwood's account of man without awareness of the Absolute (of Hinduism or any other religious thought, personal or sectarian). This is not Hell nor Purgatory (which was handled in a similar way by Bellow in *Dangling Man*): it is man's self as a purely biological mechanism with the paradoxical element of supposed understanding of psychological motives included also. George has been viewed as the exemplification of Isherwood's aim of dramatizing the objective absorption of reality by the self. With regard to this 'dramatic metaphor' Alan Kennedy has said:

> Isherwood's own temperament and trust in individual experience of self-discovery make him forego the temptation to believe in the status quo. Instead, we find at the centre of his work, not society, but a proliferation of dramatic metaphor. What might at first seem to be a question about the necessity of belonging to a group turns out to be a question of art.[1]

Here, Kennedy hints at the way in which Isherwood has carried out his study, but to study the merely stylistic, as Kennedy does in his essay, omits a more important consideration of how valuable a contribution to the modern autobiographical novel this book is. In fact, the character of George is not given any 'trust' in any form of discovery nor in the status quo. There is too much condemnation of trust in the novel, and the main scheme of the book is that we see a person begin his day as an 'it' – a mere biological object – then experience a certain critical and nervous metal life before returning to being an object at the end, with a conjectural cessation of the 'object' and all its functions. As Jonathan Raban has pointed out, there are subtle stylistic usages which, by shifting the personal pronouns at the opening of the book, make the reader analyse the 'George' object while at the same time they feel their identification with him.

Given that I read the novel as a portrait of deterministic life and humanist self-doubt, the only possible answer to the nihilistic and utterly physical imprisonment of self is a metaphor near the end of George's day where the universal omnipresence of a 'total consciousness' – the 'Atman' or Absolute – saves man from a mechanistic concept of himself in total alienation from his reality. Isherwood indicates the nature of the only comprehension open to George (and to all humanity) that even begins to answer the questions about being that modern philosophy has been preoccupied with. I will return to this at the close of this section.

We first meet a George who is a body, functioning admirably well in a routine and familiar sensual world. His mental consciousness is trivial also, and he has an obsession with wrestling with the mental pressures exerted by his neighbours. His body emerges from biological function only to that desirable specificity of the stereotype of the traditional American novel about the individual in a conformist's society. But he is primarily a homosexual who is losing his secure concept of his identity through the loss of love and companionship.

The prison of self that he becomes conscious of is concerned with the nature of individual consciousness, and this is a universal concern in twentieth-century literature, but this individualism needs an attempt at definition here, for my purposes at least. Raymond Williams has explained the problem of definition clearly and his remarks are helpful here:

> Most social psychologists now stress the way in which awareness of oneself as a separate individual has to be learned . . . . As Mead puts it, 'The self, as that which can be object to itself, is essentially a social structure, and it arises in social experience'. This definition implies different levels of individuality. To begin with, individuals have varying innate potentialities, and thus receive social influence in various ways. Further, if there is a common 'social character' or 'culture pattern', each individual's social history, his actual network of relationships, is, in fact, unique.[2]

This uniqueness of identity and what creates it in the 'network' are what Isherwood details to determine George's awareness of his need to reappraise himself. There has to be this specificity in the relationship so that George can try to understand it, though he often does so in terms of stereotypes. The heterosexual families, for instance, he knows well, but though he stereotypes them, he also feels them as unique by emphasizing names, as everyone does. As Isherwood attempts to make George an object limited by, above all, other people, he needs a sharp contrast between the *raisons d'être* of George and the others: and so the Tithonous lecture and the meeting with Charlotte are essentially confrontations where role-play is dominant and George's two selves of role-figure and 'enquiring other' come into conflict.

In order to show the contrast between George's past life with Jim and the present, Isherwood uses metaphors of play for the present life. The games, plays, gambits and rules of relationships in George's social life illustrate once again the nature and centrality of significant action for Isherwood. George's true actions ended when Jim died; all meaningful action has now gone and all that remains is role-play.

> They arrive in mixed groups – from which nearly all the boys break away at once, however, to take part in the masculine hour of the ball-playing.[3]

This more mundane level of play is mentioned to define the preoccupation of the heterosexual majority, but there is an extension of this that is important:

> Oh, by all means let them screw; if they can still cut the mustard; and if they can't, let them indulge without inhibitions in babylike erotic play.[4]

This highlights the frequent accounts of George's cynical thoughts and fantasies on the heterosexual norm. This is used to show his homosexual love and its relation to his self-concept. The 'game' of the role-play in his life is the very force that allows for George's dissent from the norm. Isherwood even extends these metaphors to comment on minorities:

> Won't he keep getting himself involved in the wrong kind of game? The game he was never born to play, against an opponent who is quick and clever and merciless?[5]

This is said of the Mexican in the long account of tennis (pp. 42–3). Here Isherwood uses an image that extends to all minorities and applies to George – as everything he reflects upon does: the games he plays as lecturer in literature, friend of Charlotte, neighbour to Mrs Strunk and so on, are doomed to failure as his only true attachment to life was through Jim. All these assaults upon the individual consciousness only serve to drive the certainty of isolation deeper. Even George's involvement with literature is part of the mendacity of life-experience as he knows it:

> The class sits staring, as it were, at the semantically prodigious word. About. What is it about? They'll say anything at all. For nearly all of them . . . still regard this business as a tiresomely ridiculous game . . . .[6]

However, the range of the novel has to go beyond the repeated criticism of the subjective experience of one social entity in a well-defined milieu, and George's consciousness actually grows gradually from the merely biological organism to the human identity imprisoned by time, space and (even more insurmountable) the action of mind and the will. We are made to follow this mental and very subjective recording of experience as it steadily assembles an extremely distorted and prejudiced view of an alien world. It is counterbalanced by George only rarely, as in his conversation with Grant, when there are hints that the subjective consciousness may not be so negative:

> An American motel room isn't a room in an hotel, it's THE room. And it's a symbol – an advertisement in three dimensions if you like – for our way of life .... The truth is, our way of life is too austere for them (the Europeans). We've reduced the things of the material plane to mere symbolic conveniences. And why? Because that's the essential first step. Until the material plane has been defined and relegated to its proper place, the mind can't ever be truly free ....[7]

This appears to be a defence of the way of life that George has confronted and hated in his routine existence. George sees it as a way of overcoming the effects of time as experienced as an enemy force by man. The implication is that America is free to exploit the spiritual life but it applies only to George himself or to a small minority. A 'symbolism' of the duties and pleasures of life is what George sees as the outcome of all the 'games' he has observed in this day in which we study his actions. Yet there is also in George (even if he is not aware of what the spiritual element in identity is) a far more significant part of the novel's material: an example of the consciousness imprisoned in time. The lecture on Tennyson's 'Tithonus' (pp. 50–55) contains many ironies which apply to his own condition:

> Where was I? Oh yes – so poor Tithonus gradually became a repulsive, immortal old man .... And Eos, with the characteristic heartlessness of a goddess, got bored with him and locked him up. And he got more and more gaga, and his voice got shriller and shriller, until suddenly one day he turned into a cicada.[8]

This could almost be a metaphorical account of the object at the opening of the novel; the creature that exists in a suspension of time after Jim's death: 'There is not a question of stopping. The creature will struggle on and on until it drops. Not because it is heroic. It can imagine no alternative'. Even in George's rare moments of physical self-awareness which deny the effects of time, the control is still hinted at:

> I am alive, he says to himself. I am alive! And life energy surges hotly through him . . . how good to be in a body. Yet he still claims a distant kinship with them (the young men).[9]

The limits of his consciousness are explained most cogently in the meeting with Charlotte; it is a contentment that asks no more than the physical:

> And now, as George pours the vodka . . . he begins to experience this utterly mysterious unsensational thing . . . not bliss, not joy – just plain happiness . . . . George's felicidad is sublimely selfish; he can enjoy it unperturbed while Charlie is in the midst of buddy-blues or a Fred-crisis.[10]

George is no more than a being totally rooted in physical satisfaction but his intellect aspires to know a kind of truth beyond this: the aspiration, Isherwood suggests, for man, is usually delusion. George attempts to deceive himself that time is not his prisoner and will ultimately win. His argument (above) concerning materialist society and the leisure for the cultivation of a 'spirituality' is unconvincing. It has been taken out of context and misread by Paul Binding[11] and this shows just how easy it is to misapprehend the themes here.

A further negative response to the understanding of time which George gives concerns the nature of man's concept and use of past time. In his conversation with Charlotte, after her sentimentality regarding England and the Old World, George is dismissive:

> 'But Geo. The Past! Surely you can't pretend you don't know what I mean by that?'
> 'The past is something that's over.'
> 'Oh really – how can you be so tiresome!'

'No Charley, I mean it. The Past is over. People make believe that it isn't, and they show you things in museums. But that's not the past. You won't find the past in England. Or anywhere else for that matter.[12]

Time and space, as impositions on consciousness and mind, are the determinants of George's perceptions in the whole scheme of the book. At the opening. 'Waking up begins with saying AM and NOW. That which has woken then lies for a while staring up at the ceiling and down into itself until it has recognised I and therefrom deduced negatively I am, I AM NOW. Here comes next.' The only momentary escapes from time and space occur when George is drunk. When very drunk with Kenny (p. 147) he sees that they are no longer in 'the symbolic-dialogue relationship'. It is only when drunk that he ceases to judge and criticize his social self and role play.

The development of the themes moves full circle as we have observed George in a typical day. He ends as a consciousness – one in millions – each enclosed in the prison of the self that isolates man.

The escape from this isolation, through what is best described as communication through conventional ways, George has learned to see as being futile; he speaks to Kenny on this:

'I know exactly what you want. You want me to tell you WHAT I KNOW.

Oh Kenneth, Kenneth, believe me – there's nothing I'd rather do! I want like hell to tell you. But I can't. I quite literally can't. Because, don't you see, WHAT I KNOW IS WHAT I AM? And I can't tell you that.[13]

The self, then, is largely constructed through social identity, but that element in self-identity forged by understood or cognitive individual experience is, for George, incommunicable. I would argue that the Existentialist problem, as so often expressed in fiction, is one of showing that communication is the only kind of action left to man: the proof of 'authenticity' of being in the world. George is a study of a man who has no capacity even for creating his own authenticity through art or communication.

Isherwood's metaphor of the rock pool exemplifies the repeated attempt in the novel to describe this individuation of experience of the self as an incommunicable thing. Time is finally incomprehensible without the effort towards the transcendent. As Helen says to Bast in *Howard's End*: 'Death destroys a man; the idea of death saves him'. But where she sees love as the saviour of man, Isherwood prefers to suggest self-understanding, however this may be achieved.

The rock pool is used to illustrate the nature of the consciousness that knows no more than the impositions of time on everyday perceptions:

> Each pool is separate and different, and you can, if you are fanciful, give them names – such as George, Charlotte, Kenny, Mrs Strunk. Just as George and the others are thought of, for convenience, as individual entities, so you may think of a rock-pool as an entity; though of course, it is not.[14]

The 'sea' that joins the rock pools and leaves them isolated at 'ebb tide' may represent many things, but if it is communication or relationships or love, then it has no answers to Isherwood's question: 'What does it mean to speak of self-identity?'. In the final section of the novel, George returns to his corporeal prison. He is the slave of time, which may put an end to him almost with a caprice. The style returns to the clinical description of physical functions:

> Thus, slowly, invisibly, with the utmost discretion and without the slightest hint to those old fussers in the brain, an almost indecently melodramatic situation is contrived: the formation of the atheromatus plaque.[15]

In the closing pages, the only hint of anything outside man is time: 'Is there, indeed, anything for them (the rock pools) to tell – except that the waters of the ocean are not really other than the waters of the pool?'. We have in the novel nothing more than the (or one of the) psychologist's conception of the self, as put by G. H. Mead:

> The essence of the self is cognitive. It lies in the internalised conversation of gestures which constitutes thinking, or in terms of which thought or reflection proceeds. And hence the origins and foundations of the self, like those of thinking, are social.[16]

Although there is much social criticism in the novel, and while humour in the book can be compared with the type found in a great deal of American fiction, in the final analysis Isherwood's main preoccupation is with the condition of a man who has no more than an incommunicable self-identity. Of course, as with Sartre's Roquentin or Beckett's Malone, George is a version of the Everyman figure, but with Isherwood's desire to concentrate on an intense study of a 'single' man – one unique self – one must relate George to Oliver or Patrick and see him as a sadly one-dimensional man and as much a captive of social relationships as Joseph K. It is interesting to note that John Barth took this theme to a ludicrously contracted form in *Lost in the Funhouse* where this style occurs to stress the perplexity of such a fictional character as 'identity':

> I see myself as a halt narrative: first person, tiresome. Pronoun sans ante or precedent, warrant or respite. Surrogate for the substantive; contentless form ... Who am I? A little crise d'identité for you.[17]

Like *A Single Man*, Barth's work here concerns the reduction of the conventionally overrated first person narrative of identifiable stereotypes to a parody of itself. Isherwood's George, seen as an 'object', is also much less the fully and conventionally convincing protagonist of the modern novel than it is possible to perceive him in the central college and party scenes.

In his last two novels, then, Isherwood has made fictional forms, original and experimental in some ways, to develop his preoccupation with the fictional study of identity into a sharp contrast: the polarities of the transcendental and the physical, non-theistic and earthbound. Although in *A Meeting by the River* Patrick was initially bound into a series of familial role-plays similar to those of George, he had the capacity to escape the restriction that the lack of any transcendental dimension may bring. Isherwood suggests that even the effort towards perception of the Absolute unity of things and other notions which may help to comprehend time and evolution is enough to find a kind of freedom from the 'death that destroys a man'. Isherwood, like Auden, found much in the American life-style and attitudes to morality that enabled a European homosexual to 'reconsider the family values and find a life outside the bourgeois one of England'. In Patrick he discussed this kind of personal revision of thought, but in George we have a mechanical habituation to sensuality and comfort. Like Dante's Belaqua (see above section on Vedanta) he knows the right way to self-knowledge but lacks the ability to take action and perceives the self as an isolated object. Therefore in the passage that contains the rock pool metaphor, the suggestion that George is merely one 'specimen' among many in the novel is one that makes it valid to see Isherwood as writing one more variation on the existential novel. What he did achieve here, however, is an original study, in fiction, of a man without self-knowledge and without the ability to 'connect' when the 'ebb tide' of time and fate leave him isolated (or, as is hinted, he actually begins to die). It is man in his most base form, but at the same time, man who knows the place of materialism and sensuality, for he knows love in some sense – and that is his tragedy. In losing Jim, he lost 'the idea of death' and so of life too.

8

Autobiography and Fiction in Isherwood's Work

Isherwood's novels illustrate many of the current critical issues concerning the nature of narrative, and yet they also show, quite outstandingly, the nature and strengths of the autobiographical novelist's art. These two facts do not lie easily together as one is complex, theoretical and uncertain, whereas the other is simple and familiar: novelists who depended almost entirely on their own diaries and journals for fictional material are numerous. Writers as different as Arnold Bennett and D. H. Lawrence rely heavily on personal experience and on writings other than novelistic ones in their preparations for their best work. Where Isherwood is particularly interesting is in the context of the study of fiction as a search for self-understanding, even, it has been said, to a narcissistic degree.

In fact, it is necessary to consider some of the fundamental elements of autobiography when studying Isherwood. Theorists agree that 'truth' and 'design' are in conflict in any autobiographical writing. The writer can never reproduce the true reflection of experience, as his overall scheme of writing about the past imposes an artificial pattern – a logic that was never there originally in life. Even in the classic autobiographies such as Rousseau's *Confessions* or Goethe's *Autobiography* there has been a stated purpose which the book relentlessly develops and explicates. The interplay of mimetic writing and history has also interested critics and theorists, and in this respect, Isherwood is an informative example.

Autobiography sets out to evaluate, to explain, to confess and, most of all, to work for truth; the truth of experience as it is later perceived. This Wordsworthian recollection in tranquillity is, of course, highly suspect. The writer will insist on understand-

103

ing his motives in youth or his follies and failings in important
stages of his life, and so on.

In Isherwood's case, various motives for his autobiographical
novels have been suggested. He was always fascinated by acting,
by role-play, the actions of the social self, etc. His early affection
for the theatre, and his lifelong passion for film indicate this:

> The cinema puts people under a microscope; you can stare at
> them, you can examine them as though they were insects
> even. True, the behaviour you see on the screen isn't natural
> behaviour; it is acting, and often very bad acting too ....[1]

Isherwood developed the habit of looking at his 'other self' in
this way, and he also inspected others closely. His novels have a
wealth of detail in terms of possessions, objects, rooms and
clothes, but mostly it is people as actors, and chiefly 'Christopher' who absorb him as a writer. So meticulous is this enquiry
into the Christopher who rebelled, travelled and wrote about
Berlin, as opposed to the Christopher who found the satisfaction of Vedanta, a gay life-style in California and peace, that the
subject of *Christopher and his Kind* is a revision of much of the
earlier *Lions and Shadows* and other shorter pieces. It is as if
Isherwood wants to cancel out an earlier self, labelling him as an
'actor' – not himself at all.

It is worth considering the religious novels in this context too.
As Peter Abbs says in an essay on Edwin Muir's celebrated
autobiography: 'The central preoccupation of autobiography is
that realisation of self is cast into doubt. Perhaps identity is only
ever a partial fragment of something larger ... unknowable?'[2]
There is a real insight here; Isherwood came to find the former 'I
am a camera' approach too distant and passive to handle such
things as higher-consciousness experience. Too often, he had
relied on irony to make his statements for him. In the American
years, he had to work hard in order to translate into novel
material such diary entries as the one of 17 November 1940,
when he recorded a reaction to saying the word, 'God': 'It
seemed to vibrate down, down into the depths of me ... and
produced a kind of echo in my consciousness'.[3]

What was happening to him, both as novelist and as student of
religion, was a growing awareness of the polarities in the larger
world of good and evil, belief and atheism, heterosexual and

gay, war and peace and so on, contrasted with the polarities within the individual. In his novels, this is often where the humour is to be found, as he was well aware of the dangers of solemnity and seriousness in religious fiction. George's explanation of Tithonus in the Huxley novel is typical of this (in *A Single Man*). The lecture is bordering on the farcical, but it is loaded towards bathos, as George's words on Tithonus actually apply to George himself. As this is written in the historical present tense, the sentimentality, and thus the significance, are played down: 'George beams at them. He does so hate unpleasantness'.[4]

Constantly, in reading the last three novels, even in the comparative blandness of *The World in the Evening*, we are reminded of the centrality of friendship and love in Isherwood's religious scheme. If the autobiographical conclusion is that we are always more than we can understand and hold, then friendship is the communication of the bond that best reflects self-knowledge. In all his novels, we have friendship; it is usually male and usually concerning the feelings of an older man for a younger; and these are not necessarily sexual relationships by any means. In Norris, Lancaster, Bergmann and George, we have the extremes of both types, but the bond of friendship is always central in the main novels. These outsider figures and minority figures create their own farcical or tragic ruin, but they have a charisma or at least a fascination for the observer. They escaped class and duty, restraint and peer-group morality. What they claimed or demanded was friendship, even when embedded in the lower forms of Vedanta 'maya'. In his autobiographical writings, Isherwood always analysed friendship, as if each important relationship was a stage in education. Often, there is a conflict of intellects, beginning with the opening discussion on art in *All the Conspirators* in which echoes of Oscar Wilde's wit are easily heard, up to the last record, where the clash of temperaments between Isherwood and his guru are described.

It may be also noted that, as one critic has said, there is 'a solipsistic circle' in Isherwood's writing which unites both fact and fiction; this may be seen as one of the central techniques in his work as a whole.

The notion here is that the 'Christopher' persona is the focal point, all data processed through his objective eye; relationships are under scrutiny and motivations thoroughly investigated. What is a crucial element in this apparent narcissism is often overlooked, however: the almost obsessive concern for self-criticism and mockery. This introspection took on its most intensive form in his journals which form the basis of virtually all his writings in all genres. Initially, even this was a pose, a posture to be observed:

> I had decided to keep a journal. It was to be modelled on Barbellion's *Diary of a Disappointed Man*. My chief difficulty was that, unlike Barbellion, I wasn't dying of an obscure kind of paralysis – though, in reading some of my more desperate entries, you would hardly suspect it: 'Too miserable to write any more . . . . All the same symptoms . . . . This is the end.'[5]

What all this demonstrates is that what is common to all his writing – fiction and autobiography – is the irony of the self-deceptions and acts of 'Christopher' who is a persona of 'Isherwood Agonistes', a combatant constantly rebelling against class, snobbery, philistinism and so on, but actually trying on the garments of new selves, fresh identities. The friendships and the solipsism are no more than this, and one may illustrate this nowhere more representatively than in *My Guru and his Disciple*. This chapter of autobiography is a comic-serious apologia for his greatest rebellion – that of leaving Britain with Auden and then dismissing many of the values and assumptions of his own mystic-intellectual circles of expatriates, going even beyond people such as Aldous Huxley and Gerald Heard in his search for alternative beliefs and new self-knowledge. In the first half of the book, Isherwood reveals, quite unashamedly, the petty provisos and qualifications, the compromises and tacit agreements that moulded his study and practice of Vedanta. The charting of what he calls 'the death of the ego' is written with such humour, innocence and confessional tone that it invites the reader's indulgence. This is familiar territory in terms of his novels also, of course.

Yet, interspersed between the self-reproaches and trivial criticisms of failures, Isherwood writes a truly convincing record of a spiritual journey, and this is often in novelistic terms. The fictional Patrick and George are reflected in the real dilemmas and questionings of a bashful noviciate, allured by a structure of values that offer the peace and the love that the restless fictional personae had been looking for. In a sense, then, reading his autobiography causes the reader to revise and review the readings of the novels that he may have experienced. The quality of this journey through discipline into routine is exemplified by the frequent discursive asides:

> How delightful religion used to be – in the days when I wasn't doing anything particular about it! What delicious emotions, what pleasantly sentimental yearnings! Now it's just a stupid boring misery. I seem to get worse and worse . . . . Swami says it's like cleaning out an inkwell which is screwed to the table: you keep pouring in water and nothing comes out but dirty old ink . . . .[6]

This tone backs up what he theorized would be in his projected religious novel, as discussed in his review of Maugham's *The Razor's Edge*:

> How am I to prove that X is not merely insane when he turns his back on the whole scheme of pleasures, rewards and satisfactions which are accepted by the Jones, the Smiths and the Browns, and goes in search of super-conscious experience? The only way I can do this is with the help of the Jones themselves.[7]

The clumsy symbolism of 'Tawel fan' in *The World in the Evening* is recognized for what it is: a glib statement which has been worked out unsatisfactorily before the novel was written.

From this example it may be observed that Isherwood's autobiography did work out, from diary notes, the requisite development in translating factual details into novelistic material. He had to take a great deal of criticism for this 'eccentric' behaviour. Even as recently as February, 1990, the critic Robert Carver has labelled Isherwood's American religious fiction as 'Mere navel-gazing' as opposed to his earlier 'Mass-Observation style writing'.[8] Critics have simply not been properly aware of the depths to which Isherwood's preparation for the writing of his highest fictional achievement took him, largely in autobiography but also in religious biography, literary journalism, travel writing and in private diaries. All this came from the same steady impulse – the spiritual journey inside himself.

Isherwood's autobiography is one of the strain between 'truth' and 'design' but it is always honest and direct in its record of a slow journey to the truth. The stances of the fictional personae, from Herr Issyvoo to George, had all shared qualities of understandable moral cowardice, but in this one finds the religious strengths. Isherwood's later seekers after enlightenment do not begin their journeys looking at a distant peak of perfection, nor of nirvana; they look around at the chaos of human life on the plain – Matthew Arnold's 'darkling plain':

> Swept with confused alarm of struggle and flight
> Where ignorant armies clash by night.[9]

The autobiographical enterprise led him to certain 'ground rules' of writing religious fiction. These were that the novel be identifiably mundane, not tinted by awe and wonder or objective, intellectual distance; that the central figure be no 'saint' and that the pulls and claims of human friendship and love be the strongest. It is too much of a simplification to assert that sensuality is the opposite of religious obedience to one's spiritual dictates. Isherwood found a hard compromise in his own life, and his protagonists have to fight harder to shed the 'maya' of the sensual world than to achieve 'the death of the ego' by prayer and study. Peter Abbs's words about autobiography being concerned with the perceptions of 'We are always and forever more than we can symbolically grasp' in the essay referred to earlier, apply as well to 'Christopher' and to the fictional characters, as they do to abstract academic study of biographical techniques.

For those diverse reasons, Isherwood's work in the novel presents one of the clearest examples of how the process of life-experience takes on its many fictional guises in multi-layered levels of meaning. In terms of criticism, it means that Isherwood's fiction may be approached through a range of very different methods. The relation of his work to the specialized theory of autobiography is not within the scope of this study, but such a critical work may be done in the future.

9
Some Critical Perspectives

Isherwood's writing career has often been seen by critics and literary historians as consisting of two distinct periods: the thirties European fiction and the post-war American fiction. Until recent full-length biographical and critical studies pointed out that his later work might be worth some consideration, the accepted view had been that the importance and the quality of his writing had declined as he insisted on scrutinizing issues of identity and homosexuality after *Prater Violet* (1946). Paul West, for instance, comments that when Isherwood tries to handle 'moral significances' he produces only 'inflated pretentiousness' and he also links Isherwood with Somerset Maugham as being 'symptomatic rather than for the exposition of any message'.[1] Similarly, Walter Allen, who had made a strong case for Isherwood as a novelist who reflected thirties concerns brilliantly, omits his American writing completely from his second major survey of the novel, *Tradition and Dream* (1986), and this is a study that sets out to survey the English novel since the end of World War II. If Isherwood has been classified as an American writer, then equally, he is noticeably absent from current surveys of American writing in that period also.

Of course, issues of the 'importance' of any particular novelist are certain to be beset by problems of criteria. Does 'important' or 'significant' imply discussion of stylistic innovation or philosophical insight? Perhaps both may be required. The virtues of Isherwood's novelistic technique in his so-called 'typical' work of the thirties have usually been those of objective socio-realism, dramatic and structural qualities (often related to film technique) and something rather vague called 'human comedy'. Included within this are complimentary remarks on his strength as a satirist and as an autobiographical novelist. What has been ignored until Paul Piazza's study[2] is his aspiration to explore

109

questions of belief and existential issues. A common attitude is
that his religious or philosophic novels are somehow of a lower
order than, for instance, Sartre or Bellow. Francis King summarizes this well when he describes Isherwood's status as being
in the 'second rank' of novelists and his case is expressed in
terms of a basic, self-defeating contradiction in Isherwood's
objectives:

> Vedanta, like other Eastern religions, teaches the necessity
> for detachment from all worldly desires and preoccupations
> and the elimination of self. It is, however, precisely in worldly
> desires and preoccupations and in the differences, attractions
> and conflicts between individual selves that the novelist has
> usually sought his material.[3]

The problem with this critical position is that it is possible to
indicate that the central exploration in all Isherwood's fiction is
that of social man, not some representative figure like the
characters of, for instance, Samuel Beckett's fiction. Beckett's
Malone Dies (1958 in Beckett's English version) is, it could be
argued, a novel that concentrates on the detached voice in isolation, the withdrawn self, far more than Isherwood's George in *A
Single Man*. Yet even Malone is plagued by images and
memories from his past. In Isherwood's novels, the protagonists
are immersed in 'desires and preoccupations' of the self. King's
condemnation is widely held in general critical opinion, but this
is a complete misunderstanding of the nature of the novels that
were written as a direct result of Isherwood's own religious
commitment. Like all issues of belief, particularly those based
on the experience of 'conversion', the dilemma for the artist or
writer expressing the self in states of awareness and questioning
is that often the language of everyday consciousness is inadequate. Therefore, as has been demonstrated in the chapter on *A
Meeting by the River*, the thematic and metaphorical elements of
a novel's structure have to be utilized.

It is necessary to clarify here exactly how Isherwood's novels
written after the admitted failure of *The World in the Evening*
(1954) demonstrate that, contrary to King's view, Isherwood
did assert important perceptions and characteristics of the individual within his social milieu and his 'solipsistic circle' as
quoted earlier. Far from being in a solipsistic strait-jacket,

unable to communicate fully or to exist in social relationships, the protagonists Oliver and George are enmeshed in bonds of affection and need between people which actually create their renunciation and isolation.

What we have, in fact, in the last two novels, is an annotated, impassioned account of isolation and withdrawal from the inescapable roles we have to fill and somehow 'inhabit' as individuals. Again, where Beckett repeatedly insists on negativity and defeat, Isherwood constantly pinpoints affection between people. That he chooses to write about homosexual characters is in many ways a bonus, as a further dimension is added to his enquiry in terms of artistic and philosophical depth.

The consistent feature of Isherwood's prose throughout his development as a novelist is the versatility of his enquiry into the significance, sharpness and vitality of what the detached observer notes and responds to. In the thirties, when travel writing was one of the most relevant and appealing genres, with its own modes of comprehending allegory, politics and a relation of autobiography to reportage, Isherwood wrote one of the most polished and readable in the form; this was the account of his journey to the Manchurian front in the Sino-Japanese War, *Journey to a War*. This is a book that shows how much he was able to comprehend the realities of political, economic and military issues as they affected ordinary lives. He uses a novelist's skills to illuminate the universal by reference to the particular. His often-noted 'tea-tabling' method and his 'cosiness' as Cyril Connolly called his affection for writing about domestic comforts, are ways of expressing the centrality of human communication in terms of affection, sharing and honesty. Few novelists have brought the minutiae of domesticity, material possessions and routine into prominence in fiction as Isherwood has done. His travel writing shows these immersions in what Joseph Conrad called 'the destructive element' often more plainly than in the fiction, where he has other purposes of characterization and so on. He was still interested in the form in 1946 when he was working on his South American book, *The Condor and the Cows*, which was published in part that year. Equally, he was aware, from the time of his earliest works, of the fleeting, unfaithful nature of the life-data of experience. On the train in China, for instance, after we have been told about food, buildings, railway stations and aeroplanes, we have the statement:

> There was a curious sense of relief, even of pleasure . . . .
> Everyday life, so complex and anxious, was soothingly
> simplified to the narrowness of a single railway track. Our
> egotisms, our ambitions, our vanities, were absorbed,
> identified utterly with the rush of the speeding train . . . a
> tunnel swallowed us into roaring darkness . . . .[4]

The critical interest here is that Isherwood is including a dimension of lyrical, impressionistic detail within an essentially
factual, businesslike and journalistic work. As in works of travel
and autobiography of the thirties in which travel literature and
the novel overlapped and influenced each other, here Isherwood is attempting to do what he succeeded in doing in the last
two novels (*A Single Man* and *A Meeting by the River*): to
chronicle the recession, the withdrawal of the social self into the
truths of the 'waters of consciousness' as he called this state at
the conclusion of *A Single Man*.

Criticism may learn a great deal from earlier misconceptions
or simplifications of a novelist's work. In Isherwood's case, one
could locate the first important critical enquiry, in which some
effort was made to evaluate the writing without total reliance on
Isherwood's biographical experiences and records, in an essay
written by John Whitehead in 1965. This essay indicated the
direction that we should take in order to understand that in
fiction, when a writer is 'thinking aloud' towards spiritual faith
or even giving some exposition of the move towards faith, it
does not necessarily mean that the novel in question must be
propaganda or mere personal indulgence. Whitehead shows the
consistency in Isherwood's work, pointing out that many of the
preoccupations of *Lions and Shadows* and of *All the Conspirators* persist, in transformations, within the narratives of the
American novels. The important, summative statement from
the essay is that 'Writing about the world from the viewpoint of
the outsider, he enables us to see the nature of our own, the
human predicament'.[5]

Although it would be entirely possible to take a critical cue
from this and relate Isherwood's work to the thesis of Colin
Wilson in his seminal work, *The Outsider* (1956), that Existential non-involvement in social conformity and expectations is
the 'key' to Isherwood's fictional themes, it should be asserted
that Isherwood's work is far closer to that of poetic expression of

experience, particularly in the later novels. It is, for example, a useful parallel to compare his work with those examples of poets' attempts to record the struggle towards faith or perception at its extremes, outstandingly in the work of the Metaphysical poets and G. M. Hopkins. More recently, also, there has been Seamus Heaney's collection *Station Island* (1984).

This may be seen in the thought behind a poem such as George Herbert's 'The Collar' in which the pull of the earthly, sensual world is in opposition to the discipline of a priest's vocation. Herbert's description of the binding of man to faith as a 'rope of sand', as the voice of his devil within puts it, is indicative of the dissolving of certainty and discipline in the form of human love (as in *A Single Man* where, in fact, we see the triumph of the temporal love over metaphysical speculation). Similarly, Herbert's speaker wishes to 'go abroad' from the confines of the 'home' of the church and of his belief. Throughout all Isherwood's writing, the call of sensuality, rebellion, individualism, etc. has always been a central part of his structure and characterization. In a sense, the Norris, Bergmann and Patrick types have been the alter-egos of the 'saints', as Isherwood used the word in his essay on the problems of the religious novel. They have been object-lessions in failure within the maya of Vedanta belief.

In more recent years, the homosexual novel has been more prominent in critical discussion as fiction has changed so radically. Some critics have found in Isherwood's work an apologia for the gay attitudes to relationships and to the status of minorities generally; also, in a more fundamental sense, they have observed a more enlightening viewpoint on heterosexual attitudes and assumptions. Some fictional explorations have been more extreme in this than the critical ones. Manuel Puig, for instance, in *Kiss of the Spiderwoman* (1976) makes use of connections between political exercise of power and sexual politics, using the gay character as a catalyst who is effective in both worlds. Copious footnotes on social biology relate fictional actions and statements to various sociological theories. By the side of this, Isherwood's supposed role as a 'homosexual novelist' or as a contributor to some quasi-revolutionary artistic movement centred in California are innocuous and entirely misled. His own statements on such labelling insist that he has simply written about a minority group. Perhaps it is more constructive in this context to point out that one characteristic of his fiction has been the imagery and settings of frontiers. His initial concept of *A Meeting by the River* as a coming-together of two different men at a boundary is typical of this. The 'boundary' or 'frontier' often relates to the moral demarcation of heterosexual and homosexual: the two states of mind are as opposite as two political states and often the characters clash on issues of trivial behaviour and attitudes. In any case, as a general comment on this placing of Isherwood as a purely 'homosexual novelist' it may be said that many great writers on war have really been making statements about peace; the same may be said in terms of homosexual writers really concerning themselves with heterosexuals.

There is certainly no evidence in his fiction of any aggressively assertive statements of gay identity and his treatment of homosexuality in the novels and stories has been remarkable in its implicit assumption that stereotypes, clichés and jargon are never evident in any linguistic register relating to such a subculture. If characters are one-sided, it is either done with a specific purpose in mind, or with admitted failure, as in the couple in *The World in the Evening*. When critics have examined 'The Homosexual as hero' in Isherwood's work, as Paul Piazza and Stephen Adams have done, the result has been largely to state what is plainly apparent: that one type of homosexual in his work is typified by Norris – arch and posturing, vulnerable yet combative – and the other type represented by George. As Piazza rightly says, George is written with directness and honesty.[6]

Most outstanding of all in this area is the depiction of the isolation of the homosexual: the loneliness that encourages the sagacity of George, in fact. His perceptions of the heterosexual world go far deeper than any of the earlier protagonists and the 'single' man of the title is a reference that is loaded with levels of irony. In its three connotations it points to the philosophy that Isherwood had developed by the end of his novel-writing. First, the homosexual is 'single' outside the familial morality of the heterosexual; second, he is alone, and last, he is universal in his one-ness: the rock pool metaphor applies to all. Biology aims at the singleness of death, in other words. Yet opinions such as 'but for the most part the private hells which Isherwood explores in many of his post-war novels have little universal human significance',[7] still appear in print.

The ultimate motivation for Isherwood's close fictional study of the homosexual protagonist has been, then, an instinctive and personally-experienced sense of the isolation of the member of such a minority. As Federico Lorca said, it was experiencing the 'macho' attitudes in his own Granada that gave him a sympathetic understanding of 'the gypsy, the negro, the Jew and the moor . . .'.[8] However, it should be stressed that it is a difficult critical task to try to place Isherwood in the Modernist niche along with such writers as Manuel Puig, despite the fact that what is often at the centre of Puig's fiction is also Isherwood's central concern as both homosexual and outsider, and as one who shared a stable domestic life with Don Bachardy, he would have also agreed with Puig that the life of the affections is primary – not the life of the cultivated senses. The Romantic view of the recognition and cultivation of sensual responses was humorously but tragically related in Isherwood's story of Mr Lancaster.

One must point out that if criticism of Isherwood's work is to progress, then it must be in the context of no restricted categorization. His work is that of a writer who tried to resolve the problems of the religious novel; and he did this with the added burden, or perhaps sometimes the impetus, of a spiritual journey of his own. Journeys always provided him with a supply of metaphors which would describe the experience of life-in-the-world which is part of Vedanta. This was always a search for dependable moral values in a world of disorder. His journey to a war was essentially no different from his journey to the peace of the *Bhagavad Gita*; and his theatrical diversion to *The Ascent of F6* with W. H. Auden was as much about overcoming hypocrisy and narrowmindedness as about politics or philosophy.

Isherwood's contribution to the novel has been principally in two main areas. First, in his period of writing up to his departure for America, he added significantly to the vibrancy and richness of socio-realism, particularly in the way that he employed some of the more dramatic elements of film technique. His vivid and telling juxtaposition of open crowd scenes with seedy interiors, placing human warmth and contact alongside the corrupt and violent world of social upheaval captured the mood of the time through the eyes of the young who wanted to question values and to express feelings of disquiet.

In his American period, it may be argued that his achieve-

ment is more important. He approached the difficulties and inherent pitfalls of writing about spiritual experience in an age
when Eastern religion was glibly and deprecatingly associated
with the Beat and Hippy movements, higher consciousness
drugs and Woodstock. In the long tradition of novels that deal
with spiritual polarities and oppositions, a list that includes
Stendhal as well as Dostoievsky, Isherwood wrote with integrity, from an autobiographical basis in which he himself had to
change and register that change before transforming it into fiction. As with most writing about religious experience, he had to
find a language and form to universalize feelings that may be
expressed very simply in detached poetic statement, but in a
novel need substantial expansion and depth of treatment. An
anonymous Aztec poem expresses the core of the problem of
the material he chose to manipulate into form:

> We but dream, like one who tumbles half asleep from bed:
> I speak only of things earthy, for no-one can speak of ought
> else.

Isherwood took the risk of failure, but the enterprise was self-
discovery, even if on most occasions, the outcome was more in
terms of human weaknesses rather than of nobility, charisma or
even tragedy. In some respects, his later work relates more
closely to the American traditions than to English ones, and
perhaps future critical study will see his religious fiction in comparison with that of Jack Kerouac and the tradition of novels on
the theme of the journey of self-discovery. However that may
be, Isherwood's work will always have the individual quality of
having a basis in the personality of an exile and a quiet, analyti-
cally-minded rebel.

Notes

1. Isherwood's Life and Work

1. Isherwood, *Kathleen and Frank* (London: Methuen, 1971), p. 267.
2. Isherwood, *Lions and Shadows* (London: Hogarth Press, 1938), p. 46.
3. Ibid., p. 60.
4. Ibid., p. 62.
5. Ibid., p. 63.
6. Samuel Hynes, *The Auden Generation* (London: Faber, 1976), p. 21.
7. Isherwood, *Lions and Shadows*, pp. 75–6.
8. Ibid., p. 78.
9. Ibid., p. 187.
10. Stephen Spender, *World within World* (London: Hamish Hamilton, 1951), p. 9.
11. Isherwood, *Christopher and his Kind* (London: Methuen, 1977), p. 10.
12. Otto Friedrich, *Before the Deluge* (London: Michael Joseph, 1972), pp. 7–8.
13. Ibid., p. 12.
14. Peter Vansittart, *Paths from a White Horse* (London: Quartet, 1985), p. 117.
15. Spender, *World within World*, p. 129.
16. Ibid., p. 131.
17. Otto Friedrich states that Brecht had a 'carefully contrived image', invariably wearing a driver's cap and a black leather jacket (Friedrich: *Before the Deluge*, p. 243).
18. Spender, *World within World*, p. 121.
19. Otto Friedrich, *Before the Deluge*, p. 306.
20. In Lehmann's book, *Christopher Isherwood: A Personal Memoir* (London: Weidenfeld and Nicolson, 1987), there are several previously unpublished letters which reveal how little he felt needed explanation. Lehmann came to reason and understand Isherwood's motives well.
21. John Lehmann, *New Writing in Europe* (London: Penguin, 1940), p. 47.
22. Ibid., p. 50.
23. H. Gustav Klaus, *The Literature of Labour* (London: Harvester, 1985), p. 162.
24. Robert Wennersten, 'An Interview with Christopher Isherwood': *Transatlantic Review* 42/43, pp. 5–20.

25. Quentin Crisp, *The Naked Civil Servant* (London: Jonathan Cape, 1968), p. 8.

26. Louis MacNiece, *The Strings are False* (London: Faber, 1965), p. 172.

27. T. C. Worsley writes about this very vividly in his novel *Fellow Travellers* (London: London Magazine Editions, 1971), pp. 15–16: 'opposite the shop was one of those grubby working-class cafes with oil-clothed tables, each with its soiled sauce-bottle on it . . . this was all the more popular with the clientele for being both working class and grubby. In those days anything working class was "in" with the left wing intelligentsia . . . .' This location is important for the two homosexual characters in the narrative. The boy-bars in Berlin were of this type.

28. Isherwood, *My Guru and His Disciple* (London: Methuen, 1980), p. 41.

29. The distortions and misapprehensions caused by the pop art connections with Eastern mysticism did not help in a proper understanding of the reality of Vedanta, of course.

30. Interview in *Transatlantic Review*, see note 24 above.

2. Early Novels

1. Isherwood, *All the Conspirators* (London: Penguin, 1976), p. 7.

2. Ibid., p. 8.

3. Philip Larkin, 'MCMXIV' in *The Whitsun Weddings* (London: Faber, 1964), p. 28.

4. Brian Finney, *Christopher Isherwood, A Critical Biography* (London: Faber, 1979), pp. 70–1.

5. Isherwood, *All the Conspirators*, p. 15.

6. Ibid., p. 6.

7. Ibid., p. 43.

8. Ibid., p. 102.

9. Ibid., pp. 143–4.

10. Isherwood, *Lions and Shadows*, p. 296.

11. Isherwood, *The Memorial* (London: Hogarth, 1960), pp. 61–2.

12. Ibid., p. 77.

13. Ibid., p. 116.

14. Ibid., pp. 90–1.

15. Ibid., p. 173.

16. Ibid., p. 133.

17. Ibid., p. 139.

18. Ibid., p. 257.

19. Isherwood, *Lions and Shadows*, p. 211.

20. Isherwood, *The Memorial*, pp. 287–8.

3. The Berlin Fiction and Documentary Writing of the 1930s

1. W. Allen, 'The Future of Fiction' in *Penguin New Writing*, ed. John Lehmann (London: Penguin, 1949), pp. 102–3.

2. See Gareth Griffiths, 'Biography' in *A Dictionary of Modern Critical Terms*, ed. Roger Fowler (London: Methuen, 1973), pp. 23–4.

3. George Orwell, *Coming up for Air* (London: Penguin, 1971), p. 13.

4. John Lehmann, *I am My Brother* (London: Longman, 1960), p. 17.

5. Isherwood, *Lions and Shadows*, p. 184.

6. Isherwood, *Christopher and his Kind*, p. 134.

7. W. I. Scobie, 'The Youth that was I' in *London Magazine*, May, 1977, pp. 23–30.

8. Quoted by A. Goldman in 'A Remnant to Escape' in M. Cunliffe (ed.), *American Literature since 1900* (London: Sphere, 1975), p. 317.

9. Isherwood, *Prater Violet*, p. 24.

10. Ibid., pp. 30–31.

11. H. Ruitenbeek, *The New Sexuality* (London: New Viewpoints, 1972), p. 92.

12. A. Kennedy, *The Protean Self* (London: Macmillan, 1974), p. 213.

13. Isherwood, *Kathleen and Frank*, p. 360.

14. Isherwood, *Mr. Norris Changes Trains*, p. 9.

15. Ibid., p. 15.

16. Ibid., p. 37.

17. Ibid., p. 53.

18. Martin Buber, *Between Man and Man* (London: Fontana, 1974), p. 42.

19. Isherwood, *Exhumations*, p. 105.

20. Isherwood, *Goodbye to Berlin*, p. 123.

21. G. S. Fraser, *The Modern Writer and his World* (London: André Deutsch, 1964), p. 137.

4. The Berlin Period: Shorter Fiction

1. Samuel Hynes, *The Auden Generation* (London: Faber, 1976), p. 181.

2. See interview with R. Wennersten, *Transatlantic Review* 42/43, p. 168.

3. Hynes, op. cit., p. 168.

4. G. Plimpton, *Writers at Work* (4th Series) (London: Penguin, 1977), p. 168.

5. John Lehmann *Thrown to the Woolfs* (London: Longman, 1981), p. 24.

6. Ibid., p. 52.

7. Isherwood, *Goodbye to Berlin*, p. 13.

8. Ibid., p. 55.

9. Ibid., p. 50.

10. Ibid., p. 52.

11. Ibid., p. 52.

12. Ibid., p. 58.

13. Ibid., p. 68.

14. Ibid., pp. 103–4.

15. Ibid., p. 138.

16. Ibid., p. 204.

17. Ibid., p. 120.

18. Emile Zola, *Thérèse Raquin*, Preface to 1868 edition, reprinted (London: Penguin, 1973), p. 22.

5. The Influence of Vedanta on the Novels

1. Stanley Poss, *London Magazine* vol. 1, no. 3, p. 42.
2. Isherwood, 'Discovering Vedanta' in *Twentieth Century* vol. 1, Autumn 1961, pp. 64–72.
3. Ibid., p. 71.
4. Isherwood, *Prater Violet*, p. 98.
5. Ibid., p. 98.
6. Ibid., p. 100.
7. H. Hesse, *Siddhartha* (London: Picador, 1973), p. 112.
8. Samuel Beckett, *The Lost Ones* (London: Faber, 1971), p. 1.
9. Isherwood, *Exhumations*, p. 137.
10. A. Swingewood and D. Laurenson, *The Sociology of Literature* (London: Paladin, 1971), p. 214.
11. Isherwood, *Exhumations*, p. 139.
12. David Daiches, *Literary Essays* (London: Oliver and Boyd, 1966), p. 212.
13. K. M. Sen, *Hinduism* (London: Penguin, 1978), p. 19.
14. Ibid., pp. 83–4.
15. *London Magazine* vol. 1., no. 3., p. 48.
16. Stuart Hampshire in *Encounter* Nov. 1962.
17. See J. Fryer, *Christopher Isherwood* (London: N.E.L., 1977), p. 251.
18. Isherwood, *Exhumations*, p. 140.
19. Colin Wilson, *Poetry and Mysticism* (London: Hutchinson, 1970), p. 97.
20. Juan Mascaro, ed., *The Upanishads* (London: Penguin, 1978), p. 13.
21. Isherwood, *The World in the Evening*, p. 1.
22. Ibid., p. 23.
23. Ibid., p. 23.
24. Ibid., p. 27.
25. Ibid., p. 32.
26. Ibid., p. 48.
27. Ibid., p. 280.
28. Ibid., p. 315.
29. Angus Wilson in *Encounter* Aug. 1954.
30. Juan Mascaro, ed., *Bhagavad Gita* (London: Penguin, 1978), p. 75.
31. J. Jebb, *London Magazine* April 1962, p. 88.
32. Samuel Beckett, *Malone Dies* (London: Penguin, 1977), p. 27.
33. Isherwood, *Down there on a Visit*, p. 46.
34. Ibid., p. 8.
35. Ibid., p. 177.
36. Isherwood, *Exhumations*, p. 121.
37. G. A. Feuerstein, *Introduction to the Bhagavad Gita* (London: Ryder, 1974), p. 88.
38. Isherwood, *Down there on a Visit*, p. 161.
39. Juan Mascaro, op. cit., p. 75.
40. Isherwood, *Down there on a Visit*, p. 174.
41. Ibid., p. 268.

42. Ibid., p. 268.

43. Aldous Huxley, *The Devils of Loudun* (London: Penguin, 1972), p. 322.

6. The Religious Novel and the Transcendental Self

1. R. Sheppard, in *A Dictionary of Modern Critical Terms* ed. by R. Fowler (London: Routledge, 1973), pp. 62–4.

2. See Ch. 1, note 24, R. Wennersten, p. 74.

3. C. S. Lewis, *Surprised by Joy* (London: Bles, 1955), p. 209.

4. C. Wilson, *The Outsider* (London: Pan, 1963), p. 278.

5. E. F. N. Jephcott, *Proust and Rilke* (London: Chatto & Windus, 1972), p. 16.

6. Ibid., p. 17.

7. Isherwood, *A Meeting by the River*, p. 38.

8. S. Maugham, *The Razor's Edge* (London: Heinemann, 1944), p. 250.

9. T. Morgan, *Somerset Maugham* (London: Heinemann, 1980), p. 483.

10. H. Hesse, *Siddhartha* (London: Picador, 1973), p. 107.

11. Isherwood, *A Meeting by the River*, p. 13.

12. Ibid., p. 20.

13. Ibid., p. 136.

14. Ibid., p. 136.

15. Ibid., p. 136.

16. K. Sen, *Hinduism* (London: Penguin, 1978), pp. 83–4.

7. 'A Single Man': The Prison of Selfhood

1. A. Kennedy, *The Protean Self* (London: Macmillan, 1974), p. 213.

2. R. Williams, *The Long Revolution* (London: Penguin, 1975), p. 100.

3. Isherwood, *A Single Man*, p. 19.

4. Ibid., p. 26.

5. Ibid., p. 43.

6. Ibid., p. 54.

7. Ibid., p. 76.

8. Ibid., p. 53.

9. Ibid., p. 87.

10. Ibid., pp. 103–4.

11. See review of 'Imagining America', Paul Binding, *New Statesman* vol. 99, no. 2568, p. 866. 'Isherwood thus praises America's most castigated features – its material overabundance, its lack of social cohesion etc. because he feels they are all conducive to a new kind of spirituality'. This is a statement by George: so, trust the tale, not the teller.

12. Isherwood, *A Single Man*, p. 119.

13. Ibid., p. 149.

14. Ibid., p. 155.

15. Ibid., p. 157.

16. Ibid., p. 156.
17. J. Barth, *Lost in the Funhouse* (London: Secker and Warburg, 1969), p. 35.

8. Autobiography and Fiction in Isherwood's Work

1. Isherwood, *Lions and Shadows*, p. 53.
2. Peter Abbs, 'Autobiography: Quest for Identity', in B. Ford (ed.), *The Pelican Guide to English Literature* vol. 8, p. 53.
3. Isherwood, *My Guru and His Disciple*, p. 63.
4. Isherwood, *A Single Man*, pp. 52–3.
5. Isherwood, *Lions and Shadows*, p. 59.
6. Isherwood, *My Guru and His Disciple*, pp. 142–3.
7. Isherwood, *Exhumations*, p. 138.
8. See *New Statesman* 12–1–1990, p. 38.
9. Matthew Arnold, 'Dover Beach'.

9. Some Critical Perspectives

1. P. West, *The Modern Novel* (London: Hutchinson, 1973), pp. 78–9.
2. P. Piazza, *Christopher Isherwood: Myth and Anti-Myth* (New York: Columbia University Press, 1978).
3. Francis King, *Christopher Isherwood* (London: Longman, 1976), p. 24.
4. Auden and Isherwood, *Journey to a War* (London: Faber, 1938), p. 188.
5. John Whitehead, 'Christophananda: Isherwood at 60' in *London Magazine* (vol. 5, no. 4, July 1965), pp. 90–100.
6. Piazza, op. cit., pp. 191–2.
7. Gilbert Phelps, 'The Post War English Novel' in *The Pelican Guide to English Literature* (vol. 8, ed. B. Ford) 1983, pp. 417–49.
8. Ian Gibson, *The Assassination of Federico Garcia Lorca* (London: Penguin, 1983), p. 23.

Select Bibliography

Isherwood's Principal Writings

All The Conspirators (1928)
The Memorial (1932)
Mr. Norris Changes Trains (1935)
In collaboration with W. H. Auden:
The Dog Beneath the Skin (1935)
The Ascent of F6 (1936)
On the Frontier (1938)
Journey to a War (1939)
Isherwood, cont. *Goodbye to Berlin* (1939)
Prater Violet (1945)
The World in the Evening (1954)
Down there on a Visit (1962)
An Approach to Vedanta (1963)
A Single Man (1964)
Exhumations (1966)
A Meeting by the River (1967)
Kathleen and Frank (1971)
Christopher and his Kind (1977)
My Guru and his Disciple (1980)

Selected Criticism

(Place of publication is London unless indicated.)

Cyril Connolly, *Enemies of Promise* (André Deutsch, 1938)
V. Cunningham, *British Writers of the 1930s* (O.U.P., 1988)
Brian Finney, *Christopher Isherwood: A Critical Biography* (Faber, 1979)
Jonathan Fryer, *Isherwood: A Biography of Christopher Isherwood* (N.E.L., 1977)
Samuel Hynes, *The Auden Generation* (Faber, 1979)
Francis King, *Christopher Isherwood* (Longman, 1976)
Paul Piazza, *Christopher Isherwood: Myth and Anti-Myth* (New York, 1978)
Alan Wilde, *Christopher Isherwood* (New York, 1971)
There is a bibliography of Isherwood's works, published Los Angeles, 1968, covering 1923–67 (California State College).

A Glossary of Hindu Terms

Atman   Self. In the epic writings, *The Upanishads*, it is pointed out that Brahman and Atman are the same. The spirit expresses himself in every soul. Religious students in Isherwood's situation have to understand the dictum: 'Thou art That'.

Bhakti   Prayer and devotion.

Brahman   The all-pervading God.

Jnana   Knowledge.

Karma   Action or service for others.

Vedanta   A philosophy that is mostly based on the study of the Hindu epic, *The Upanishads*.

The *Bhagavad Gita* and *The Upanishads* are sources of much of the Eastern thought that Isherwood studied and tried to live by. The *Gita* dates from between the 5th and 2nd centuries B.C. being a part of the epic *Mahabharata*. Its concern with pacifism (as Isherwood saw) was relevant to Isherwood's personal dilemma at the time of his first reading it. *The Upanishads* date from about 700 B.C. and are of less importance in understanding the background to Isherwood's Vedanta studies.

Index

125